WILLIAMS-SONOMA

New American Cooking

California

GENERAL EDITOR **Chuck Williams**

RECIPES AND TEXT **Janet Fletcher**

FOOD PHOTOGRAPHY **Leigh Beisch**

TIME
LIFE
BOOKS

New Amer[ic...]

The Pacific Northwest

Th[e...]

California

The Southwes[t...]

...an Cooking

Heartland

New England

The South

Table of **Contents**

Introduction

When I moved to California from Texas to go to college in the mid-1970s, I had never tasted a fresh artichoke, never eaten with chopsticks, and never heard of radicchio. Little did I know that good cooking was a passion in my new state, and that it would become my passion, too.

By 1980, the notion of a "California cuisine" had taken hold. Magazine editors used the phrase to describe what they viewed as a culinary breath of fresh air, an approach to cooking that celebrated the seasonal and the local. Chefs used it to define their style, even if they all had a different vision of what it meant.

Two decades later, the phrase has greater meaning and validity than ever. In many ways, the more we celebrated California cuisine, the more there was to celebrate—more farmers' markets; better wine, bread, and cheese; and more awareness of the rewards of seasonal cooking.

This book is a snapshot of California cuisine today, a rich but restless subject that will shift as soon as my shutter clicks. Every region's cooking evolves, but I think California's evolves faster because of the influx of immigrants and the open minds of the audience. Every day new restaurants open and new cooks arrive on our shores. But right now, at the dawn of the millennium, certain hallmarks of California cuisine are indisputable.

Seasonality California cooks not only acknowledge the seasons, they revel in them. They resist hot-house tomatoes and wait for the local crop. When figs, persimmons, or other short-season crops are at hand, few shoppers leave a farmers' market without them.

Ethnic diversity One in four Californians is an immigrant whose own culinary traditions are shaping the food choices for the rest of us. Instead of grabbing a fast-food hamburger for lunch, a software designer in San Jose or an aeronautical engineer in Los Angeles could easily choose Vietnamese *pho* (beef noodle soup), Thai curry, Indian tandoori chicken, Mexican tacos, or Salvadoran *pupusas*.

Appreciation for artisans While the artisan-food movement is nationwide now, it clearly started in California with people like Sonoma County goat-cheese maker Laura Chenel and La Brea Bakery's Nancy Silverton in Los Angeles. These people and many others have revived Old World ways of making bread, cheese, wine, and olive oil.

Mediterranean spirit Many California cooks draw inspiration from the cooking of the Mediterranean. We have the wine, the olive oil, the tomatoes, the coastline. We have so many similarities of agriculture and climate that dishes from southern France, Italy, Spain, and Greece seem completely at home on our tables.

A health-conscious sensibility California is, after all, the land of Dr. Dean Ornish and his 10-percent-calories-from-fat diet; pencil-thin Hollywood starlets; and, I would wager, more vegetarians and "almost vegetarians" than any other state.

Of course, these hallmarks did not develop overnight. Indeed, it's safe to say that this fortunate state has always had a distinctive cuisine, in part because of the immigrant presence, and in part because the varied geography and felicitous climate produce the raw materials that inspire good cooking.

Immigration Matters

The contribution of California's immigrants cannot be overstated. The early Italian Americans started cheese businesses, developed the fishing industry, and built many of the wineries that stand today. The Chinese worked the shrimp boats, opened restaurants, and established major Chinatowns in San Francisco, Oakland, and Los Angeles. With their greengrocers, fish markets, and noodle manufacturers, these communities-within-communities have kept Asian cooking vital in California.

In recent years, immigrants from Southeast Asia have expanded our culinary horizons, introducing us to fish sauce, lemongrass, coriander roots, fresh turmeric, and galangal—items now found in mainstream California markets. Hispanic newcomers have taught us to know and love fresh and dried chiles, black beans, queso fresco, and salsa.

Immigration statistics tell more of the story. In the 1950s, almost half of California's immigrants were European. Today, about 90 percent come from Asia, Mexico, or Central America—a huge ethnic shift. Amazingly, one-third of the nation's immigrants live in California. No wonder the state's cuisine is so open armed and multicultural.

Available at market from March through May, California artichokes (opposite) are a harbinger of spring. Seared beef and Asian greens (left) is a prime example of Asian influences on California cuisine.

Blessed by Geography

With a thousand miles of coast-line on the west and the massive Sierra Nevada on the east, California's varied microclimates and geography support a remarkably diverse agriculture.

For fifty years, the state has been the nation's number-one agricultural producer, with nearly one-third of its acreage devoted to farming. It provides half of the country's fruits, nuts, and vegetables. For several crops—almonds, artichokes, dates, figs, kiwifruits, olives, persimmons, pistachios, prunes, raisins, and walnuts—it is virtually the exclusive producer.

In balmy Southern California, growers nurture heat-loving crops such as avocados, grapefruits, oranges, and dates. In the cooler coastal areas around Monterey, farmers concentrate on crops such as artichokes, broccoli, brussels sprouts, cauliflower, and lettuces. The San Joaquin Valley is home to table grapes, stone fruits, and tomatoes; farther north, in the Sacramento Valley, growers cultivate rice, prunes, and walnuts. And of course, the Napa and Sonoma Valleys yield world-famous wine grapes.

Milk, cheese, and livestock are also among California's chief farm products. In recent years, several small producers have found viable niches in these commodity businesses. Niman Ranch organic

From the foggy Pacific coast to the sunny inland valleys, California's many microclimates produce a rich variety of crops. Wine grapes (below) and almonds (opposite) are two primary ones.

fish, as well as squid, swordfish, and albacore tuna. The southern harvest includes mackerel, squid, sardines, bonito, swordfish, shark, spiny lobster, halibut, prawns, and sea cucumbers. Oyster farms in Northern California and abalone farms near Monterey add to the choices. There's even caviar from Sacramento River sturgeon.

To me, what's most exciting about California cuisine today is the passion for great ingredients. Increasingly, producers are trying to understand the factors that contribute to quality, whether they're pressing olives for olive oil, making sheep's milk cheese, or growing Zinfandel grapes. And increasingly, cooks are rewarding that quality, seeking it out, shunning the tasteless, and showing that they are willing to pay more for food grown sustainably and with flavor foremost. For those who love California and want its culinary reputation to grow, such attitudes suggest a bright future.

beef, Straus Family organic milk, and Caseificio Gioia cheeses prove you don't have to be big to succeed.

A Seafood Feast

As for that long stretch of coastline, it supports a fishing industry that keeps California cooks supplied year-round with fresh seafood. About three hundred varieties of fish and shellfish are caught in our state's waters, from Crescent City in the north to San Diego in the south.

Northern waters yield sea urchins, Dungeness crabs, salmon, pink shrimp, and groundfish. Along the central coast, fishermen bring in several species of sole and rock-

BÛCHE
MADE BY JUNIPER GROVE FR[...]
GOATS' MILK. RICH, SOFT, CREAM[...]
A LITTLE PUNGENT.
$7.70 $4.00 HAL[...]

1 Appetizers, Soups & Salads

Seasonal ingredients shine in many of California's favorite first courses, such as a salad of heirloom tomatoes with balsamic vinaigrette (page 48), a summery white corn chowder (page 30), or one of spring's jumbo artichokes stuffed with focaccia crumbs (page 36). In homes, an appetizer may be as simple as a bowl of warm baked olives (page 42) or toasted almonds (page 18) to accompany the evening's first glass of California wine. In restaurants, appetizers and salads are so popular among health-conscious Californians that many diners make a meal of them. Who wouldn't be satisfied with a baked goat cheese salad (page 35) followed by red pepper and tomato soup (page 24)?

Toasted Almonds with Sea Salt

2 cups (11 oz/345 g) whole
unskinned almonds

1 tablespoon extra-virgin olive oil

1 teaspoon sea salt

There's no better match for a bottle of California Chardonnay than these nutty slow-roasted almonds. Baking them slowly drives off moisture and makes them particularly crisp. I buy unskinned almonds because I believe they are fresher, but you can use blanched almonds and omit step 2.

1. Preheat the oven to 325°F (165°C).

2. Bring a saucepan three-fourths full of water to a boil over high heat. Add the almonds and boil for 30 seconds. Drain, then immediately wrap the almonds in a kitchen towel and rub them in the towel to loosen the skins. Pinch the almonds from the skins; the almonds should slip out easily.

3. Transfer the almonds to a heavy rimmed baking sheet. Add the oil and toss to coat evenly. Add the salt and toss again.

4. Place in the oven and toast, stirring the almonds once or twice so they brown evenly, until golden brown and fragrant, about 30 minutes. Transfer to paper towels to cool completely, about 1 hour, before serving.

MAKES 2 CUPS (11 OZ/345 G)

NUTRITIONAL ANALYSIS PER ¼ CUP SERVING
Calories 125 (Kilojoules 525); Protein 4 g; Carbohydrates 4 g; Total Fat 12 g;
Saturated Fat 1 g; Cholesterol 0 mg; Sodium 248 mg; Dietary Fiber 2 g

Potato and Roasted Garlic Soup

1 whole head garlic

1 teaspoon olive oil

¼ cup (2 oz/60 g) unsalted butter

1 large yellow onion, minced

2 lb (1 kg) russet potatoes, peeled and cut into large chunks

2 cups (16 fl oz/500 ml) chicken stock

2 cups (16 fl oz/500 ml) water

1 bay leaf

1¾ cups (14 fl oz/430 ml) milk, or as needed

salt and freshly ground pepper to taste

3 tablespoons thinly sliced fresh chives

Garlic cloves become soft and mild when roasted whole. Here, the aromatic cloves are added to a creamy potato soup to give it a flavor boost. Look for heavy garlic heads with large, firm cloves and no sooty spots. Serve this soup as a first course, followed by roast pork with steamed chard.

1. Preheat the oven to 400°F (200°C). Put the head of garlic on a sheet of aluminum foil and drizzle with the olive oil. Seal the foil around the garlic to make a package. Bake until the garlic is fragrant and the cloves feel soft, about 40 minutes. You will need to unwrap the package to check for doneness; if the cloves are still firm, reseal and continue baking. When done, set aside to cool. When cool, peel the cloves; they should slip easily from their skins. Set aside.

2. Meanwhile, in a large saucepan over medium heat, melt the butter. Add the onion and sauté, stirring, until soft, about 10 minutes. Add the potatoes, stock, water, and bay leaf and bring to a simmer. Cover, adjust the heat to maintain a gentle simmer, and cook until the potatoes are tender, about 25 minutes. Remove the bay leaf and discard.

3. Working in batches, transfer the potato mixture to a food processor or blender and add the garlic cloves. Secure the lid and cover with a kitchen towel. Process until completely smooth. Return to a clean saucepan and stir in 1¾ cups (14 fl oz/430 ml) milk, or enough to thin the soup to your taste. Season with salt and pepper and reheat gently over medium heat.

4. Divide the soup among warmed bowls. Garnish with the chives, dividing evenly. Serve immediately.

SERVES 6

NUTRITIONAL ANALYSIS PER SERVING
Calories 264 (Kilojoules 1,109); Protein 7 g; Carbohydrates 34 g; Total Fat 12 g; Saturated Fat 7 g; Cholesterol 31 mg; Sodium 382 mg; Dietary Fiber 3 g

Every July, nearly 120,000 people descend on the central California town of Gilroy for a three-day celebration of garlic. During this long weekend, they consume truckloads of the "stinking rose" in such dishes as stuffed mushrooms and pasta with pesto. Judges select the best garlic recipes in a consumer cooking contest, and hundreds of volunteers work for a wage that they donate to local charities.

Launched in 1979, the Gilroy Garlic Festival has generated so much publicity that Gilroy now proudly proclaims itself the Garlic Capital of the World. Some credit the media coverage with helping America's fresh garlic consumption almost triple between 1988 and 1997.

Today, California produces nearly 90 percent of the domestic crop, growing more than 500 million pounds (250 million kg). Perhaps three-quarters of the crop is dehydrated for garlic salt, garlic powder, and processed foods. But the rest is savored fresh in home kitchens and restaurants.

In California, commercial garlic is planted in the fall from individual cloves. The sprouting cloves produce straplike leaves that resemble leeks,

Garlic Galore

with the bulb maturing underground. When the leaves begin to turn yellow in summer, farmers stop watering the plants. When the tops are dry, the garlic is pulled and dried in the sun for a week or more. Then the tops are trimmed and the bulbs sorted and readied for shipping to garlic lovers throughout the country and around the world.

Romaine Hearts with Caesar Dressing

DRESSING

3 tablespoons mayonnaise

5 or 6 anchovy fillets

1 large clove garlic, chopped

6 tablespoons (3 fl oz/90 ml) olive oil

2 tablespoons fresh lemon juice,
   or to taste

salt and freshly ground pepper to taste

2 cups (4 oz/125 g) crustless bread
   cubes (½-inch/12-mm cubes)

1 tablespoon olive oil

1½ lb (750 g) trimmed romaine
   (cos) lettuce hearts or 3 heads
   romaine lettuce, pale hearts only

1 cup (4 oz/125 g) shredded Vella dry
   jack cheese (use medium holes on
   a four-sided grater)

To give Caesar salad a California twist, replace Parmesan with nutty dry jack. Legend has it that this cheese was created by accident, when a San Francisco wholesaler put some Monterey jack in storage during World War I and forgot about it. When the war interrupted shipments of Italian Parmigiano, he remembered his cheese, which had aged to golden perfection.

1. Preheat the oven to 350°F (180°C).

2. To make the dressing, in a blender or small food processor, combine the mayonnaise, anchovies, and garlic and purée until smooth. With the motor running, add the oil in a slow, steady stream to make a thick sauce. Gradually add the 2 tablespoons lemon juice. Taste and add more if desired. Season with salt and pepper and process again. Transfer to a bowl and set aside.

3. In a bowl, toss the bread cubes with the olive oil. Spread on a heavy baking sheet and bake until lightly browned and crisp, about 25 minutes.

4. Cut or tear the romaine leaves into bite-sized pieces and place in a large salad bowl. Toss with enough of the dressing to coat the leaves lightly. Taste and adjust the seasonings. Add the croutons and ⅔ cup (2½ oz/75 g) of the cheese and toss again.

5. Divide among salad plates. Top each portion with some of the remaining cheese. Serve immediately.

SERVES 6

NUTRITIONAL ANALYSIS PER SERVING
Calories 334 (Kilojoules 1,403); Protein 10 g; Carbohydrates 14 g; Total Fat 28 g;
Saturated Fat 7 g; Cholesterol 26 mg; Sodium 398 mg; Dietary Fiber 2 g

Roasted Red Pepper and Tomato Soup

2 lb (1 kg) red bell peppers (capsicums)

½ lb (250 g) plum (Roma) tomatoes

3 tablespoons olive oil

1 yellow onion, chopped

2 large cloves garlic, minced

2 teaspoons sweet paprika

2 cups (16 fl oz/500 ml) chicken stock

1 cup (8 fl oz/250 ml) water

½ cup (4 fl oz/120 ml) heavy (double) cream

salt to taste

2 tablespoons chopped fresh dill

In late summer, when sweet peppers and tomatoes are at their best, launch a meal with this creamy soup that makes the most of them. Look for red peppers that feel heavy for their size. They will have the thick, meaty walls necessary to give body to the soup.

1. Preheat the broiler (griller). Cut the peppers in half lengthwise and remove the stems, seeds, and ribs. Place, cut sides down, on a baking sheet. Place the whole tomatoes alongside. Broil (grill), turning the tomatoes as needed, until the skins of the peppers and tomatoes blacken and blister. Remove from the broiler, drape the peppers and tomatoes with aluminum foil, and let cool for 10 minutes, then peel away the skins. Chop the peppers coarsely. Chop the tomatoes finely, capturing their juices.

2. In a frying pan over medium heat, warm the olive oil. Add the onion and sauté, stirring, until soft, about 10 minutes. Add the garlic and paprika and sauté for 1 minute to release the garlic's fragrance. Add the tomatoes and their juices and cook, stirring, until soft, 3–5 minutes.

3. Working in batches, combine the onion-tomato mixture and the roasted peppers in a food processor and purée until smooth. With the motor running, gradually add the chicken stock and water through the feed tube, processing until smooth. Add ¼ cup (2 fl oz/60 ml) of the cream and the salt and process to combine. Pass the purée through a sieve placed over a bowl, pressing on the solids with a rubber spatula.

4. Pour the purée into a saucepan and heat gently over medium-low heat. Meanwhile, in a small bowl, whisk the remaining ¼ cup (2 fl oz/ 60 ml) cream until thickened but supple enough to drizzle.

5. Ladle the hot soup into warmed bowls. Using a small wire whisk, drizzle each portion with some of the lightly whipped cream. Top each serving with an equal amount of the dill. Serve immediately.

SERVES 6

NUTRITIONAL ANALYSIS PER SERVING
Calories 194 (Kilojoules 815); Protein 3 g; Carbohydrates 14 g; Total Fat 15 g;
Saturated Fat 6 g; Cholesterol 27 mg; Sodium 348 mg; Dietary Fiber 3 g

Black Bean Soup with Salsa

Make this soup the centerpiece of a Cal-Mex supper: start with a romaine (cos) salad with radishes and queso fresco and finish with oranges and cookies from a Mexican bakery.

1. Pick over the beans, discarding any stones, and rinse well. Place in a bowl with water to cover by 1 inch (2.5 cm) and let stand overnight.

2. In a large pot over medium heat, combine the vegetable oil and bacon. Cook, stirring occasionally, until the bacon softens and renders some of its fat, about 5 minutes. Add the onion and sauté until soft, 5–10 minutes. Add the garlic and sauté for 1 minute to release its fragrance.

3. Drain the beans and add to the pot along with the 6 cups (48 fl oz/ 1.5 l) water. Bring to a simmer, cover, and simmer gently until the beans are almost tender, 45–60 minutes.

4. While the beans are cooking, in a small, dry frying pan over medium heat, toast the cumin seeds until fragrant, about 3 minutes. Transfer to a mortar or spice grinder and grind to a powder. Using the large holes on a grater-shredder, grate the halved tomatoes, discarding the skins.

5. Add the cumin and the tomatoes to the beans and cook, covered, until the beans are completely tender, about 30 minutes longer. Working in batches if necessary, transfer about 3 cups (21 oz/655 g) of the soup solids to a food processor or blender along with enough of the liquid to achieve a purée. Process until smooth and stir into the remaining soup. If the soup is still too thin, purée another 1 cup (7 oz/220 g). Season with salt. Reheat gently to serving temperature.

6. To make the salsa, in a small bowl, stir together the tomatoes, onion, cilantro, chile, lime juice, and water. Season with salt.

7. Divide the soup among warmed bowls. Top each with a drizzle of sour cream and a spoonful of salsa. Pass the remaining salsa.

SERVES 8

NUTRITIONAL ANALYSIS PER SERVING
Calories 359 (Kilojoules 1,508); Protein 15 g; Carbohydrates 42 g; Total Fat 15 g;
Saturated Fat 7 g; Cholesterol 20 mg; Sodium 102 mg; Dietary Fiber 9 g

2¼ cups (1 lb/500 g) dried black beans

1 tablespoon vegetable oil

4 slices bacon, cut crosswise into pieces ¼ inch (6 mm) wide

1 large yellow onion, minced

3 cloves garlic, minced

6 cups (48 fl oz/1.5 l) water

½ teaspoon cumin seeds

½ lb (250 g) plum (Roma) tomatoes, halved lengthwise and seeded

salt to taste

½ cup (4 fl oz/125 ml) sour cream thinned with water

FOR THE SALSA
⅓ lb (155 g) plum (Roma) tomatoes, halved, seeded, and finely diced

½ small yellow onion, finely diced

¼ cup (⅓ oz/10 g) chopped fresh cilantro (fresh coriander)

½ jalapeño chile with seeds, minced

juice of ½ lime

1 tablespoon water

salt to taste

Quesadillas with Queso Fresco and Rajas

4 poblano chiles or 2 green bell
peppers (capsicums)

5 tablespoons (3 fl oz/80 ml)
vegetable oil

1 large yellow onion, halved and
thinly sliced

1 large clove garlic, minced

1 jalapeño chile, seeded and minced
(optional)

salt and freshly ground pepper to taste

6 flour tortillas, each 10 inches
(25 cm) in diameter

3 cups (12 oz/375 g) shredded queso
fresco

6 tablespoons (⅓ oz/10 g) chopped
fresh cilantro (fresh coriander)

The secret to superb quesadillas is to have the oil and pan
hot when you add the tortilla. The blast of heat will crisp it,
providing a contrast with the creamy cheese and soft rajas
(strips of roasted peppers and onions). If you can't find
queso fresco, a fresh Mexican cheese, substitute mozzarella.

1. Preheat the broiler (griller). Cut the chiles or bell peppers in half
lengthwise and remove the stems, seeds, and ribs. Place, cut sides down,
on a baking sheet. Broil (grill) until the skins blacken and blister. Remove
from the broiler, drape with aluminum foil, and let cool for 10 minutes,
then peel away the skins. Cut lengthwise into strips ¼ inch (6 mm) wide.

2. In a large frying pan over medium-low heat, warm 1 tablespoon of
the vegetable oil. Add the onion and sauté until soft, about 15 minutes.
Do not allow to brown. Add the garlic and the jalapeño chile, if using, and
sauté for 1 minute to release the garlic's fragrance. Stir in the poblano
chiles or bell peppers and season with salt and pepper. Cook, stirring, for
about 5 minutes to blend the flavors. Remove from the heat. If the mixture has thrown any juices, drain it in a sieve. Set the mixture aside.

3. In a large frying pan over medium-high heat, warm 2 teaspoons
of the oil. When very hot, add 1 tortilla and reduce the heat to medium.
Sprinkle half the surface with ½ cup (2 oz/60 g) of the cheese, keeping
the cheese away from the edges so it doesn't melt in the pan. Top the cheese
evenly with one-sixth of the pepper and onion mixture and 1 tablespoon
of the cilantro. Fold the untopped half over the filling, pressing gently.
Move the quesadilla into the center of the frying pan and cook until the
bottom is nicely browned, about 1 minute. Using a spatula, carefully turn
and cook until the other side is nicely browned, about 1 minute longer.

4. Serve immediately, whole or cut into 4 wedges. Repeat with the
remaining ingredients, using 2 teaspoons of the oil for each tortilla.

SERVES 12 AS A FIRST COURSE OR 6 AS A MAIN COURSE

NUTRITIONAL ANALYSIS PER FIRST-COURSE SERVING
Calories 249 (Kilojoules 1,046); Protein 8 g; Carbohydrates 20 g; Total Fat 15 g;
Saturated Fat 6 g; Cholesterol 20 mg; Sodium 335 mg; Dietary Fiber 2 g

Mesclun Salad with Persimmons and Pears

VINAIGRETTE

3 tablespoons walnut oil

1 tablespoon sherry vinegar

1 shallot, minced

salt and freshly ground pepper to taste

¼ lb (125 g) mesclun (baby salad greens)

2 heads Belgian endive (chicory/ witloof), halved lengthwise, cored, and cut crosswise into slices ½ inch (12 mm) thick

1 Fuyu persimmon

1 pear such as Comice, Bosc, or Bartlett (Williams)

In season, California fruits add appeal to green salads, making a dish that many of us eat almost daily seem fresh and inviting. Ripe pears and Fuyu persimmons (the kind that are tomato-shaped and firm when ripe) are among the fruits that can enhance autumn salads. If you like, add a little crumbled blue cheese.

1. To make the vinaigrette, in a small bowl, whisk together the walnut oil, vinegar, shallot, salt, and pepper. Let stand for 30 minutes to allow the shallot flavor to mellow.

2. In a large salad bowl, combine the salad greens and endive. Peel and quarter the persimmon. Slice each quarter thinly crosswise and add to the salad. Quarter, core, and peel the pear. Slice the quarters lengthwise, halving the slices if they are long. Add to the salad. Add just enough of the vinaigrette to coat the leaves lightly (you may not need it all) and toss gently. Taste and adjust the seasonings.

3. Transfer to a large platter or individual plates. Position some of the fruit slices on the surface of the salad(s). Serve immediately.

SERVES 4

NUTRITIONAL ANALYSIS PER SERVING
Calories 135 (Kilojoules 567); Protein 1 g; Carbohydrates 11 g; Total Fat 11 g; Saturated Fat 1 g; Cholesterol 0 mg; Sodium 5 mg; Dietary Fiber 2 g

W hen the first bulk baby-lettuce mixes showed up in California markets in the late 1980s, I looked at them in amazement. Who would buy these six-dollar-a-pound salad greens?

The pioneers in precut salad, as it's now called, were imitating the French mesclun, an improvisational mix of fresh-cut young greens from the kitchen garden. I recall visiting a small urban farm that specialized in the greens. The baby lettuces were hand-washed and then hand-dried.

Today, at a leading company like Earthbound Farm, the process is more mechanized and better policed for food safety. Launched in 1984, with 2½ acres (1 hectare) in Carmel Valley, the company now farms 4,800 organic acres (2,000 hectares), an increase that reflects the growth in this industry.

To make its mixes, Earthbound Farm grows perhaps twenty different salad ingredients, such as (pictured left to right from top) frisée, mizuna, romaine (cos), tat-soi, arugula (rocket), radicchio, mustard, and baby spinach. After mixing, washing, and drying, the greens are shipped in bulk boxes or packed in sophisticated plastic bags that allow

Growing Baby **Lettuces**

oxygen to enter and carbon dioxide to leave. This specialized packaging has helped the industry grow by extending the shelf life of these salads.

Today, although the head-lettuce business is far from endangered, it seems that precut is where the growth is. California consumers are happy to pay more for the convenience of prewashed and mixed greens.

White Corn Chowder

4–6 ears of white corn, husks and
 silk removed

¼ cup (2 oz/60 g) unsalted butter

½ large yellow onion, minced

1 large celery stalk, minced

1 lb (500 g) russet potatoes, peeled
 and cut into ½-inch (12-mm) cubes

2 cups (16 fl oz/500 ml) chicken stock

1 cup (8 fl oz/250 ml) water

1½ teaspoons minced fresh thyme

1 cup (8 fl oz/250 ml) half-and-half
 (half cream)

salt and freshly ground pepper to taste

3 tablespoons thinly sliced fresh chives

White corn goes quickly at California's farmers' markets
because customers like its exceptional tenderness. And for city
dwellers who don't have gardens, corn picked the day before—
or sometimes early the same morning—is a real treat.

1. Holding each ear of corn by its pointed end, and steadying its stalk
end on a cutting board, cut down along the ear with a sharp knife to
strip off the kernels, turning the ear with each cut. You will need 4 cups
(1½ lb/750 g) corn kernels.

2. In a large saucepan over medium heat, melt the butter. Add the
onion and celery and sauté until soft, about 10 minutes. Add the potatoes,
stock, water, and thyme and bring to a simmer. Cover, adjust the heat to
maintain a gentle simmer, and cook until the potatoes are almost tender,
about 8 minutes. Add the corn, cover, and continue to simmer gently
until the corn is tender, 3–5 minutes longer.

3. Transfer about 4 cups (1½ lb/750 g) of the soup solids to a food
processor along with enough of the stock to achieve a purée. Secure the
lid and cover with a kitchen towel. Process until smooth and return to
the pan. Stir in the half-and-half and season with salt and pepper.

4. Reheat gently over medium-low heat. Ladle into warmed soup bowls
and garnish with the chives, dividing evenly. Serve immediately.

SERVES 6

NUTRITIONAL ANALYSIS PER SERVING
Calories 291 (Kilojoules 1,222); Protein 7 g; Carbohydrates 38 g; Total Fat 14 g;
Saturated Fat 8 g; Cholesterol 35 mg; Sodium 381 mg; Dietary Fiber 5 g

Artisan
Cheeses

Thanks to the marvelous artisan cheeses being made in California today, it's a fine time to be a cheese enthusiast. I could easily put together a tantalizing all-California selection: Laura Chenel's Taupinière, a goat cheese that reaches perfection when properly ripened; Emily Thomson's hand-molded goat cheeses from Ventura County; Ig Vella's dry jack, an aged cow's milk cheese with a cocoa-dusted rind that rivals Parmigiano Reggiano in complexity; and anything from Bellwether Farms, where Cindy Callahan, a lawyer-turned-cheese-maker, and her son Liam make irresistible Tuscan-style sheep's milk cheeses and a fresh, molten cow's milk cheese called Crescenza.

Chenel was clearly, unknowingly, pioneering an artisan-cheese movement when she walked into Chez Panisse, the famous Berkeley restaurant, with her first goat cheeses in the early 1980s. Her success inspired others, most of them intent on making handmade cheeses based on European models.

Today, companies such as Cypress Grove, Redwood Hill Farm, and Yerba Santa Goat Dairy thrive in California, producing cheeses that merit comparison to any in France, a country long known for its fine cheese making. Cypress Grove's Humboldt Fog, a goat cheese with a layer of ash in the middle, is an impeccable example of the cheese maker's art. Redwood Hill's aged goat crottin and Yerba Santa's aged goat cheeses also impress cheese professionals.

In the Italian tradition, Caseificio Gioia, near Whittier, produces ricotta, fresh mozzarella, and burrata, a cream-filled mozzarella. Joe and Mary Matos, of the Matos Cheese Factory in Santa Rosa, make a lovely Portuguese-style cow's milk cheese called St. George that has many fans. The tangy, soft-ripened teleme from Peluso Cheese Company in Los Banos is a California original with a long history. And the Cacique Cheese Company in City of Industry makes Mexican-style cheeses such as panela, Oaxaca, and queso fresco that meet the needs of the state's Latino communities.

The cheese marketers at the California Milk Advisory Board say Junipero Serra, the same Franciscan father who brought olives and wine to the state, introduced dairy cows and cheese making, too. They date the popular Monterey jack from 1882, when a Monterey businessman began marketing a cheese developed from old mission recipes. To my taste, the best thing that ever happened to Monterey jack was when a San Francisco wholesaler put some in storage and forgot about it. Much later, he discovered the cheese, well aged, nutty, and sweet. Dry jack was born.

A California creamery displays a variety of artisan cheeses (opposite). Draining whey (below) to make Olema Valley Rounds at the Cowgirl Creamery.

Fresh Mozzarella with Roasted Peppers

4 large bell peppers (capsicums), preferably 2 red and 2 yellow

4 tablespoons (2 fl oz/60 ml) extra-virgin olive oil

4 large cloves garlic, minced

salt and freshly ground pepper to taste

1 tablespoon capers, chopped if large

1 tablespoon red wine vinegar

2 tablespoons chopped fresh flat-leaf (Italian) parsley

½ lb (250 g) fresh whole-milk mozzarella cheese

Around the state, some enterprising cheese makers and restaurant chefs have mastered the technique of stretching warm curd into mozzarella. When freshly made, mozzarella deserves to be showcased—with tomatoes and basil; with the finest olive oil and coarse salt; or with a juicy mélange of roasted peppers.

1. Preheat the broiler (griller). Cut the bell peppers in half lengthwise and remove the stems, seeds, and ribs. Place, cut sides down, on a baking sheet. Broil (grill) until the skins blacken and blister. Remove from the broiler, drape the peppers loosely with aluminum foil, and let cool for 10 minutes, then peel away the skins. Cut lengthwise into strips ¼ inch (6 mm) wide.

2. In a large frying pan over medium heat, warm 3 tablespoons of the olive oil. Add the garlic and sauté for 1 minute to release its fragrance. Add the bell pepper strips and season with salt and pepper. Stir to coat with the seasonings. Cook until the peppers are hot throughout, about 3 minutes, then remove from the heat. Stir in the capers and vinegar and transfer to a bowl. Let stand at room temperature for at least 1 hour or as long as 4 hours to allow the flavors to blend. Just before serving, add the parsley and stir to mix. Taste and adjust the seasonings.

3. Slice the mozzarella ¼ inch (6 mm) thick. Arrange the slices on a platter and sprinkle with salt and pepper. Drizzle with the remaining 1 tablespoon olive oil. Spoon the peppers alongside and serve.

SERVES 4

NUTRITIONAL ANALYSIS PER SERVING
Calories 335 (Kilojoules 1,407); Protein 13 g; Carbohydrates 8 g; Total Fat 28 g; Saturated Fat 11 g; Cholesterol 50 mg; Sodium 329 mg; Dietary Fiber 2 g

Baked Goat Cheese Salad

Popularized by Berkeley's Chez Panisse Café, goat cheese salads have become a signature of the California table. Chefs have given them their own stamp, varying the greens or the seasonings, but most of these efforts continue to showcase the affinity between warm, creamy goat cheese and crisp croutons.

VINAIGRETTE

1 shallot, minced

1 tablespoon red wine vinegar

1 teaspoon Dijon mustard

3 tablespoons walnut oil

salt and freshly ground pepper to taste

⅔ cup (2½ oz/75 g) walnuts

2 heads butter (Boston) lettuce

½ lb (250 g) fresh goat cheese

2 tablespoons extra-virgin olive oil, plus extra for the baking sheet

8 slices coarse country bread, roughly 4 by 2 inches (10 by 5 cm) by ½ inch (12 mm) thick

2 tablespoons thinly sliced fresh chives

1. Preheat the oven to 350°F (180°C).

2. To make the vinaigrette, in a small bowl, whisk together the shallot, vinegar, and mustard. Whisking constantly, gradually pour in the walnut oil to form an emulsion. Season with salt and pepper. Let stand for 30 minutes to allow the shallot flavor to mellow.

3. Spread the walnuts on a baking sheet and toast until lightly colored and fragrant, about 15 minutes. Remove from the oven, let cool, and then chop coarsely. Turn the oven to broil (grill) and position a rack about 8 inches (20 cm) from the heat source.

4. Remove the butter lettuce leaves down to the pale, crisp hearts, reserving the outer leaves for another use. Rinse and dry thoroughly, then tear into bite-sized pieces. Place in a large bowl. Using a length of dental floss held taut between two hands, cut the cheese into eight 1-oz (30-g) slices.

5. Using the 2 tablespoons olive oil, lightly brush both sides of each bread slice. Place on a baking sheet and broil (grill), turning once, until lightly toasted, about 3 minutes total. Remove from the broiler. Add the walnuts to the lettuce and drizzle with the vinaigrette. Toss well, then taste and adjust the seasonings. Divide among large salad plates.

6. Lightly oil a baking sheet. Put the cheese on the prepared baking sheet and broil on one side until soft to the touch, 2–3 minutes. With a spatula, immediately top each toast with a slice of warm cheese. Put 2 toasts on each salad plate. Garnish with the chives and serve.

SERVES 4

NUTRITIONAL ANALYSIS PER SERVING
Calories 595 (Kilojoules 2,499); Protein 19 g; Carbohydrates 35 g; Total Fat 44 g; Saturated Fat 12 g; Cholesterol 26 mg; Sodium 576 mg; Dietary Fiber 3 g

Focaccia-Stuffed Artichokes

4 large artichokes

1 lemon, halved

about 10 oz (315 g) herbed focaccia, processed into fine crumbs (about 4 cups)

½ cup (2 oz/60 g) freshly grated Parmesan cheese

¼ cup (⅓ oz/10 g) minced fresh flat-leaf (Italian) parsley

2 cloves garlic, minced

¼ cup (2 fl oz/60 ml) olive oil

salt and freshly ground pepper to taste

boiling water, as needed

In spring, when jumbo artichokes flood California's markets, many people make a meal of them. Tuck a stuffing of seasoned focaccia crumbs between their leaves and you have a substantial lunch or the centerpiece of a meatless dinner.

1. Preheat the oven to 375°F (190°C).

2. To trim each artichoke, cut off the stem flush with the bottom and rub the cut surface with a lemon half. With a serrated knife, cut about 1 inch (2.5 cm) off the top of each artichoke and rub the cut surfaces with lemon. Using scissors, cut off the pointed tips of the leaves. Gently pry open the artichoke leaves without breaking them, loosening the artichoke enough for you to reach the center choke easily. With a spoon or melon baller, scoop out the prickly inner leaves and hairy choke and discard. Squeeze the lemon halves into a large bowl of cold water and submerge the trimmed artichokes in the water as each one is done to prevent the cut surfaces from browning.

3. In a large bowl, combine the focaccia crumbs, Parmesan cheese, parsley, garlic, and olive oil. Stir well. Season with salt and pepper.

4. Drain the artichokes and pat dry. Fill the center cavities with stuffing, then use your fingers to tuck the remaining stuffing between the leaves. The innermost leaves will be too tightly joined, but the outer leaves can be gently separated and stuffing tucked between them.

5. Stand the artichokes upright in a baking dish just large enough to hold them. Add boiling water to the dish to a depth of ½ inch (12 mm). Cover with parchment (baking) paper, then with aluminum foil. Bake until tender when pierced, 50–60 minutes. Uncover, raise the heat to 400°F (200°C), and bake for about 15 minutes longer to crisp the top crumbs.

6. Transfer to a platter or individual plates and serve warm, not hot.

SERVES 4

NUTRITIONAL ANALYSIS PER SERVING
Calories 441 (Kilojoules 1,852); Protein 19 g; Carbohydrates 49 g; Total Fat 21 g; Saturated Fat 5 g; Cholesterol 13 mg; Sodium 742 mg; Dietary Fiber 10 g

Smoked Trout, Fennel and Arugula Salad

DRESSING

2½ tablespoons extra-virgin olive oil

1 tablespoon fresh lemon juice

1 small shallot, minced

salt and freshly ground pepper to taste

1 fennel bulb

1 whole boneless smoked trout,
 about ½ lb (250 g)

⅓ lb (5 oz/155 g) young arugula
 (rocket) leaves, without thick
 stems

salt and freshly ground pepper to taste

Californians adore artful salads, compositions that go beyond leafy greens to incorporate crisp raw vegetables and often smoked or otherwise cured fish or meat. A salad such as this one might be served as a first course or, in larger portions, as a light lunch. Pair it with a California Sauvignon Blanc or Pinot Gris.

1. To make the dressing, in a small bowl, whisk together the olive oil, lemon juice, shallot, salt, and pepper. Let stand for 30 minutes to allow the shallot flavor to mellow.

2. Trim off the stems and feathery tops from the fennel bulb and remove any bruised, thick, or fibrous outer stalks. Quarter lengthwise, then thinly slice the quarters crosswise. Set aside.

3. Skin the trout and break the meat up into large flakes, removing any small bones that may have been missed during processing. In a small bowl, toss the trout gently with 1 tablespoon of the dressing.

4. In a large bowl, combine the arugula and fennel. Add the remaining dressing and toss to coat evenly. Season with salt and pepper. Divide the arugula and fennel among salad plates. Arrange the trout over the greens. Serve immediately.

SERVES 4

NUTRITIONAL ANALYSIS PER SERVING
Calories 198 (Kilojoules 832); Protein 14 g; Carbohydrates 4 g; Total Fat 14 g;
Saturated Fat 3 g; Cholesterol 13 mg; Sodium 617 mg; Dietary Fiber 1 g

Salade Niçoise with Fresh Tuna

Summer is prime time for California's albacore tuna and for the green beans, potatoes, and tomatoes that complete this salade Niçoise.

1. To make the vinaigrette, in a small bowl, whisk together the vinegar, mustard, and shallot. Whisking constantly, gradually pour in the olive oil. Whisk in the capers, salt, and pepper. Set aside for 30 minutes to mellow.

2. Preheat the broiler (griller) and position a rack 8 inches (20 cm) from the heat source. Rub the tuna on both sides with the oil and place on a baking sheet. Season with salt and pepper. Broil (grill), without turning, until done to your taste, 3–4 minutes for medium. Set aside to cool.

3. Bring a saucepan three-fourths full of salted water to a boil over high heat. Add the beans and boil until just tender, 5–10 minutes. Drain, place under cold running water to stop the cooking, drain again, and pat dry.

4. In a large saucepan, combine the potatoes with salted water to cover by 1 inch (2.5 cm). Bring to a boil over high heat, adjust the heat to maintain a gentle simmer, and cook until easily pierced with a knife, 15–20 minutes. Drain and let cool.

5. At serving time, put a tuna steak on one-half of each plate. Spoon 2 teaspoons vinaigrette over each steak, then make an X on top with 2 anchovy fillets. Put 2 lettuce leaves alongside the tuna. In a bowl, toss the green beans with enough of the vinaigrette to coat lightly. Season with salt and pepper. Divide among the plates, arranging them in a bundle on the lettuce. Slice the potatoes ¼ inch (6 mm) thick, place in the same bowl, and toss gently with enough vinaigrette to coat lightly. Season with salt and pepper. Divide among the plates, arranging them alongside the beans. Divide the tomatoes among the plates, putting them alongside the potatoes. Drizzle with the remaining vinaigrette. Put 2 egg quarters on each plate. Scatter the olives over the vegetables. Serve immediately.

SERVES 6

NUTRITIONAL ANALYSIS PER SERVING
Calories 722 (Kilojoules 3,032); Protein 48 g; Carbohydrates 50 g; Total Fat 38 g;
Saturated Fat 6 g; Cholesterol 168 mg; Sodium 649 mg; Dietary Fiber 6 g

VINAIGRETTE

2 tablespoons red wine vinegar

2 teaspoons Dijon mustard

1 large shallot, minced

½ cup (4 fl oz/125 ml) extra-virgin olive oil

1½ tablespoons coarsely chopped capers

salt and freshly ground pepper to taste

6 tuna steaks, each about 6 oz (185 g) and a scant ½ inch (12 mm) thick

2 tablespoons extra-virgin olive oil

salt and freshly ground pepper to taste

1 lb (500 g) green beans, trimmed

3 lb (1.5 kg) small boiling potatoes

12 anchovy fillets

12 butter (Boston) lettuce leaves

3 small tomatoes, cut into wedges

3 hard-boiled eggs, quartered lengthwise

4 dozen Niçoise olives

Spinach, Orange and Beet Salad

4 small (but not baby) beets, about
   ½ lb (250 g) total weight, trimmed
   leaving 1 inch (2.5 cm) of stem

2 large navel or blood oranges

¾ lb (375 g) baby spinach, stems
   removed

DRESSING

3 tablespoons extra-virgin olive oil

1 tablespoon fresh lemon juice,
   or to taste

1 shallot, minced

salt and freshly ground pepper to taste

California's plump, sweet navel oranges turn up frequently in winter salads—and not just in fruit salads. They add appealing color and tang to this mix of beets and spinach, a good prelude to a main course of pork chops or duck. Red-fleshed blood oranges would also work here.

1. Preheat the oven to 375°F (190°C). Put the beets in a baking dish and add water to a depth of ¼ inch (6 mm). Cover and bake until the beets are tender when pierced, 45–60 minutes.

2. Meanwhile, cut a slice off the top and bottom of 1 orange to expose the fruit. Stand the orange upright on a cutting surface and thickly slice off the peel in strips, cutting around the contour of the orange to expose the flesh. Holding the orange over a bowl, cut along either side of each section to free it from the membrane, letting the section drop into the bowl. Repeat with the remaining orange. Put the spinach in a large bowl.

3. To make the dressing, in a small bowl, whisk together the olive oil, 1 tablespoon lemon juice, shallot, salt, and pepper. Let stand for 30 minutes to allow the shallot flavor to mellow.

4. When the beets are ready, remove from the oven and let cool until they can be handled. Peel and cut into wedges about the size of the orange sections. Put the beet wedges in a bowl and toss with just enough of the dressing to coat them lightly.

5. Using a slotted spoon, transfer the orange sections to the bowl holding the spinach. (Reserve any collected juice for another use.) Add the remaining dressing and toss to coat. Taste and adjust the seasonings, adding more lemon juice if desired.

6. Divide the spinach and oranges among individual plates. Top each serving with an equal amount of the beets. Serve immediately.

SERVES 6

NUTRITIONAL ANALYSIS PER SERVING
Calories 108 (Kilojoules 454); Protein 2 g; Carbohydrates 11 g; Total Fat 7 g;
Saturated Fat 1 g; Cholesterol 0 mg; Sodium 52 mg; Dietary Fiber 3 g

Warm Baked Olives with Garlic and Fennel

1 cup (5 oz/155 g) Niçoise olives

¼ cup (2 fl oz/60 ml) extra-virgin olive oil

2 large cloves garlic, sliced

½ teaspoon fennel seeds, coarsely crushed in a mortar or spice grinder

1 tablespoon fresh lemon juice

A daylong stay in a garlicky marinade infuses olives with flavor, and warming them intensifies the flavor even more. Serve these olives as a cocktail nibble along with toasted almonds with sea salt (page 18). If you can't find Niçoise olives, substitute Kalamata olives or even green Picholines.

1. Rinse the olives well and pat thoroughly dry.

2. In a frying pan over medium heat, warm the olive oil. Add the garlic and heat until fragrant and just starting to color, about 1 minute. Stir in the olives and fennel seeds and cook until the olives are hot throughout, about 2 minutes. Remove from the heat and let cool. Stir the lemon juice into the cooled olives and transfer to a tightly covered container. Let stand for at least 8 hours or as long as 24 hours at room temperature, shaking the container occasionally to redistribute the seasonings.

3. To serve, preheat the oven to 350°F (180°C). Put the olives and their marinade in a baking dish and bake until they are warm throughout, about 10 minutes.

4. Using a slotted spoon, lift the olives out of the marinade and transfer to a serving dish. Serve warm, not hot.

SERVES 6

NUTRITIONAL ANALYSIS PER SERVING
Calories 122 (Kilojoules 512); Protein 2 g; Carbohydrates 2 g; Total Fat 13 g; Saturated Fat 1 g; Cholesterol 0 mg; Sodium 284 mg; Dietary Fiber 2 g

W hen the Spanish missionaries arrived in California over two centuries ago, they brought more than religion. At every mission they founded, they planted olive trees, some of which still stand. What is known today as the Mission olive may or may not be the same variety that the friars planted, but it is the cornerstone of the state's huge canned olive industry.

From thirty-five thousand acres (14,170 hectares) of olive trees in its warm inland valleys, California's canneries produce three-quarters of the ripe olives consumed in the United States. But in truth, the word *ripe* is a misnomer. The olives are picked green, lye-cured to remove their natural bitterness, and oxygenated to turn them from green to black.

Compared to the canning industry, the olive oil business in California is small but rapidly changing. In recent years, several entrepreneurs have taken steps to make the state as well known for its olive oil as it is for its wine. Importing the best French and Italian trees, they have established plantings—mostly in Northern California—and sought international advice on how to make

Olives and **Olive Oil**

top-quality extra-virgin oil. The California Olive Oil Council, founded in 1992, has established a certification program to ensure that California oils labeled "extra virgin" meet international standards. High land costs mean California probably will never be a major producer, but some of the high-priced boutique oils are earning acclaim.

Thai-Style Squid Salad

2 lb (1 kg) squid

2 tablespoons peanut oil

2 large cloves garlic, minced

2 large shallots, thinly sliced

1 teaspoon red pepper flakes

¼ cup (2 fl oz/60 ml) fresh lime juice

3 tablespoons Thai or Vietnamese
fish sauce

2 teaspoons sugar

½ English (hothouse) cucumber,
halved lengthwise, seeded, and
thinly sliced

1 small red (Spanish) onion, quartered,
then thinly sliced

1 tablespoon minced fresh lemongrass

¼ cup (⅓ oz/10 g) coarsely chopped
fresh mint

24 fresh Asian basil leaves, torn into
small pieces

several lettuce leaves

Many California diners have come to know this pungent salad at neighborhood Thai restaurants. With Asian basil, fish sauce, and lemongrass increasingly available in supermarkets, people can now easily make the salad at home.

1. To clean each squid, pull the head from the body. Cut off the tentacles and discard the head. Press the base of the tentacles to force out the "beak," and reserve the tentacles. With your finger, pull out any interior matter from the body, including the quill-like cartilage, then peel off the mottled skin that covers the outside. Cut the body crosswise into rings ½ inch (12 mm) wide.

2. Bring a large pot three-fourths full of water to a boil over high heat. Add the squid rings and tentacles and cook just until they turn white, about 15 seconds. Drain and immediately rinse with cold running water. Drain well and set aside.

3. In a small frying pan over medium heat, warm the peanut oil. Add the garlic, shallots, and red pepper flakes and sauté for about 1 minute to soften the shallots and release the garlic's fragrance. Remove from the heat and add the lime juice, fish sauce, and sugar, stirring to dissolve the sugar.

4. In a large bowl, combine the squid, cucumber, red onion, lemongrass, mint, and basil. Add the garlic-shallot mixture and toss well. Taste and adjust the seasonings.

5. Line a serving platter with lettuce leaves, then spoon the salad over the lettuce. Serve immediately.

SERVES 6

NUTRITIONAL ANALYSIS PER SERVING
Calories 195 (Kilojoules 819); Protein 20 g; Carbohydrates 12 g; Total Fat 7 g;
Saturated Fat 1 g; Cholesterol 275 mg; Sodium 355 mg; Dietary Fiber 1 g

Shellfish and Avocado Cocktail

¾ lb (375 g) large shrimp (prawns),
    peeled, deveined, and cut into
    ½-inch (12-mm) pieces

½ lb (250 g) sea scallops, quartered

about 1½ cups (12 fl oz/375 ml)
    fresh lime juice

1 tomato, halved, seeded, and diced

1 small avocado, pitted, peeled, and
    diced

½ white onion, minced

¼ cup (⅓ oz/10 g) chopped fresh
    cilantro (fresh coriander)

1 large clove garlic, minced

2 tablespoons extra-virgin olive oil

1½ teaspoons dried oregano

1 jalapeño or 2 serrano chiles,
    minced, including seeds

1½ cups (12 fl oz/375 ml) tomato
    juice, chilled

salt to taste

This refreshing seafood cocktail—a variation of ceviche—is popular in California's Mexican restaurants. It is often served in a large parfait glass, but a martini glass makes a more contemporary presentation. Note that the shellfish needs to marinate for at least twelve hours.

1. In a glass or stainless-steel bowl, combine the shrimp, scallops, and enough lime juice just to cover them. Cover and refrigerate, stirring occasionally, until the shellfish has turned opaque all the way through, indicating that the lime juice has "cooked" it, 12–24 hours.

2. Just before serving, drain the shellfish, reserving the lime juice. Return the shellfish to the bowl and add the tomato, avocado, onion, cilantro, garlic, and olive oil. Add the oregano, crumbling it between your fingers to release its fragrance. Add the minced chile to taste, then add the tomato juice. Toss to mix. Season with salt. Taste and add as much of the reserved lime juice as needed to give the mixture a refreshing tang.

3. Divide among stemmed glasses and serve.

SERVES 6

NUTRITIONAL ANALYSIS PER SERVING
Calories 189 (Kilojoules 794); Protein 17 g; Carbohydrates 10 g; Total Fat 10 g;
Saturated Fat 1 g; Cholesterol 83 mg; Sodium 356 mg; Dietary Fiber 1 g

On the short list of foods that I would consider for my last meal, avocado would be near the top. With rustic bread, coarse salt, and a lemon, a ripe Hass avocado would satisfy me completely. I could eat the whole thing with no thought of calories. I would smear the smooth, buttery flesh on bread and savor every bite.

Clearly I'm not alone in thinking of the avocado as a forbidden fruit, an item too rich, too calorie-laden to eat with abandon. A recent industry ad campaign battled that very attitude with a humorous spin on the tag line: "It's Not Wrong to Be in Love with the Avocado."

In fact, the avocado has little saturated fat and plenty of nutrients. A New World native, avocados thrive in California between San Luis Obispo and the Mexican border, where sixty thousand acres (24,300 hectares) yield 95 percent of the nation's crop. Although at least seven varieties are cultivated, most growers concentrate on the pebbly-skinned Hass.

About six thousand California growers harvest avocados, so you can see that most orchards aren't large. A single tree can produce up to 60 pounds (30 kg)—about 120

California **Avocados**

avocados—a year. Luckily for the growers, avocados store well on the tree, so there's no mad rush at harvesttime. In fact, the longer they hang, the more oil content—and, therefore, more flavor—they develop. And those little fruits that some markets label "cocktail avocados"? They are miniature pit-free fruits that inexplicably develop on the trees.

Heirloom Tomatoes with Balsamic Vinaigrette

3 tablespoons extra-virgin olive oil

1 tablespoon balsamic vinegar

1 large shallot, minced

salt and freshly ground pepper to taste

1–1¼ lb (500–625 g) heirloom tomatoes, preferably a variety of colors and sizes

One of the most encouraging developments on California's family farms is the interest in "heirloom" produce—fruit and vegetable varieties from an earlier time. Many of these varieties have lost favor commercially because they don't ship or store well, but they often have superior flavor. At California's farmers' markets, it's not uncommon to find two dozen different heirloom tomatoes in a multitude of colors and sizes.

1. In a small bowl, whisk together the oil, vinegar, shallot, salt, and pepper. Let stand for 30 minutes to allow the shallot flavor to mellow.

2. Core the tomatoes. Halve them vertically if large, then slice thinly or cut into thin wedges. Halve cherry tomatoes or baby pear tomatoes, if you like. Arrange the sliced tomatoes on a platter, mixing the colors attractively. Top with the small tomatoes. Spoon the vinaigrette over the tomatoes and serve.

SERVES 4

NUTRITIONAL ANALYSIS PER SERVING
Calories 117 (Kilojoules 491); Protein 1 g; Carbohydrates 6 g; Total Fat 11 g;
Saturated Fat 2 g; Cholesterol 0 mg; Sodium 11 mg; Dietary Fiber 2 g

2 Seafood, Poultry & Meats

In times past, shrimp were so plentiful in San Francisco Bay that some restaurants gave them away. Today, the Pacific Ocean is more restrained in its gifts, but California's seafood fans still know they can count on a year-round supply of fresh fish and shellfish from nearby waters, such as king salmon, sand dabs, squid, Dungeness crabs, halibut, and tuna, all featured here. Chicken is a mainstay, of course, but poussin and duck appear on many dinner-party menus. For red-meat lovers, the state's chefs continue to devise contemporary presentations, such as seared beef and Asian greens (page 80) or grilled pork with grilled plum sauce (page 61). In many California homes, grilled lamb with Zinfandel marinade (page 58) is the essence of summer.

Steamed Mussels with Lemongrass

¼ cup (2 fl oz/60 ml) peanut oil

½ cup (2½ oz/75 g) minced shallot

¼ cup (1 oz/30 g) finely minced lemongrass

8 cloves garlic, thinly sliced

2 tablespoons peeled and finely minced fresh ginger

2 serrano chiles, minced, including seeds

2 cans (14 fl oz/440 ml each) unsweetened coconut milk

½ cup (¾ oz/20 g) minced fresh cilantro (fresh coriander) leaves and stems

2 tablespoons Thai or Vietnamese fish sauce

3 lb (1.5 kg) mussels, well scrubbed and debearded

1 large handful fresh Asian or regular fresh basil leaves

These luscious mussels are steamed in a creamy coconut-milk sauce infused with flavors characteristic of Thai cooking: lemongrass, shallots, fish sauce, and chiles. To mince lemongrass, use only the bulb portion, before the leaves branch. Remove the tough outer layers, then mince the heart.

1. In a large, heavy pot over medium heat, warm the peanut oil. Add the shallot, lemongrass, garlic, ginger, and chiles and sauté for 2–3 minutes to soften these aromatics and release their fragrance. Add the coconut milk, cilantro, and fish sauce and cook, stirring, until the mixture comes to a simmer. Adjust the heat to maintain a gentle simmer and cook until the flavors are blended, 1–2 minutes.

2. Add the mussels, discarding any that do not close to the touch, cover, and raise the heat to medium-high. Cook, shaking the pot occasionally to redistribute the mussels, until the mussels open, 3–4 minutes. Uncover and stir in the basil.

3. Divide the mussels and their liquid among individual bowls, discarding any mussels that failed to open. Serve immediately.

SERVES 4 AS A MAIN COURSE OR 6 AS A FIRST COURSE

NUTRITIONAL ANALYSIS PER MAIN-COURSE SERVING
Calories 648 (Kilojoules 2,722); Protein 18 g; Carbohydrates 19 g; Total Fat 59 g; Saturated Fat 40 g; Cholesterol 28 mg; Sodium 612 mg; Dietary Fiber 1 g

Broiled Poussins with Arugula Salad

MARINADE

3 tablespoons extra-virgin olive oil

1 teaspoon Dijon mustard

1 teaspoon fennel seeds, coarsely crushed in a mortar or spice grinder

1 teaspoon black peppercorns, coarsely crushed in a mortar or spice grinder

¼ teaspoon red pepper flakes

1 clove garlic, minced

2 poussins or Cornish hens, about 1¼ lb (625 g) each

salt to taste

¼ lb (125 g) baby arugula (rocket) or spinach, tough stems removed

¼ lb (125 g) cherry tomatoes, halved, or quartered if large

2 lemon quarters

In summer, I would buy the vegetables for this salad at a farmers' market, such as the Ferry Plaza market in San Francisco. There, shoppers are likely to find not just cherry tomatoes, but tiny red currant tomatoes, yellow pear tomatoes, and the bright orange, cherry-sized Sun Gold tomatoes— all beautiful additions here.

1. To make the marinade, in a small bowl, whisk together the oil, mustard, fennel seeds, black pepper, red pepper flakes, and garlic. Set aside.

2. Rinse the birds and pat dry. Place each hen, breast side down, on a work surface. With kitchen scissors or poultry shears, cut from the neck to the tail along both sides of the backbone; lift out the backbone. Turn breast side up and, using the heel of your hand, press down on the breastbone to flatten it. Cut off the wing tips and discard. Put the hens in a dish just large enough to hold them and coat with the marinade. Let stand for 1 hour at room temperature, turning once.

3. Preheat the broiler (griller) and position a rack 8–10 inches (20–25 cm) from the heat source. Preheat the broiler pan until very hot.

4. Season the hens well with salt on both sides. Put the hens on the broiler pan, skin side down. Broil (grill) until browned and sizzling, about 12 minutes. Remove from the broiler and collect any drippings in the broiler pan. Turn the hens, baste with the drippings, and return to the broiler. Broil, skin side up, until the skin is well browned and the juices run clear, about 8 minutes longer. Remove from the broiler.

5. Divide the greens evenly between 2 plates. Place the hens directly on the greens. Drizzle the exposed greens on each plate with about 2 teaspoons drippings from the broiler pan. Scatter the tomatoes over the greens. Squeeze the lemon quarters over all. Serve immediately.

SERVES 2

NUTRITIONAL ANALYSIS PER SERVING
Calories 774 (Kilojoules 3,251); Protein 55 g; Carbohydrates 6 g; Total Fat 58 g;
Saturated Fat 14 g; Cholesterol 312 mg; Sodium 214 mg; Dietary Fiber 2 g

Sand Dabs with Meyer Lemon and Capers

2 Meyer lemons

2 sand dabs, about ½ lb (250 g) each

salt and freshly ground pepper to taste

about ½ cup (2½ oz/75 g) all-purpose
  (plain) flour

2 teaspoons olive oil

2 teaspoons plus 3 tablespoons
  unsalted butter

2 tablespoons chopped capers

1 tablespoon minced fresh flat-leaf
  (Italian) parsley

Sand dabs are typically cooked on the bone, which keeps them intact and contributes to their excellent flavor. If you prefer, you can substitute petrale sole fillets, but they will cook faster.

1. Cut a slice off the top and bottom of 1 lemon to expose the flesh. Stand the lemon upright on a cutting board and, using a sharp knife, thickly slice off the peel in strips, cutting around the contour of the fruit to expose the flesh. With the knife, cut along both sides of each lemon section to free it. Cut the sections into small, neat dice. Using the second lemon, squeeze enough juice to measure 1 tablespoon.

2. Season the sand dabs generously with salt and pepper. Spread the flour on a plate, then dip each fish in the flour, coating both sides. Shake off the excess flour and put the fish on a rack.

3. Heat a large nonstick frying pan over medium-high heat. Add the olive oil to the hot pan. When the oil is hot, add the 2 teaspoons butter. When the butter melts, foams, and just begins to color, add the fish. Reduce the heat to medium. Cook on the first side until it is well browned and the fish are cooked halfway through, 3–4 minutes, depending on their size. Turn the fish gently with a spatula. Cook on the second side until the fish are no longer pink at the bone, 3–4 minutes longer. Remove the fish to a warmed platter.

4. Pour off any fat in the pan and return to low heat. Add the remaining 3 tablespoons butter to the pan along with the diced lemon, lemon juice, capers, and parsley. Swirl the pan until the butter melts. Pour over the fish and serve at once.

SERVES 2

NUTRITIONAL ANALYSIS PER SERVING
Calories 528 (Kilojoules 2,218); Protein 46 g; Carbohydrates 24 g; Total Fat 29 g; Saturated Fat 14 g; Cholesterol 166 mg; Sodium 570 mg; Dietary Fiber 1 g

Although it has been culti-vated in California since the early 1900s, the deli-cate, sweet-scented Meyer lemon has only recently come into its own. For years it was mainly a backyard fruit with no commercial presence. But when contemporary California chefs began to celebrate the locally grown, they rediscovered the Meyer and sparked demand for this unusual citrus.

Discovered in China by an American agricultural explorer in 1908, the Meyer lemon has a mysterious family tree. Some say it may be a cross between a lemon and a mandarin orange. Whatever its parentage, its lemon-orange flavor enhances seafood, asparagus, ice cream, and cake.

Compared to the two most common lemons in California, the Eureka and the Lisbon, the Meyer has a thinner skin with a richer yellow-orange color. Scratch that skin and you release a powerful—and appealing—floral fragrance. Inside, it has tender walls and a goodly amount of low-acid juice.

In fact, if chefs have one complaint about the Meyer, it's that it is not tart enough for some preparations.

Meyer **Lemons**

Where tartness is desirable—say, in vinaigrettes—they may supplement Meyer lemon juice with some con-ventional lemon juice or vinegar.

Thanks to the renewed interest in Meyer lemons, a few commercial growers have planted them. But Meyers are still rare enough in the marketplace that Californians who love them often plant their own.

Grilled Lamb with Zinfandel Marinade

1 boneless leg of lamb, about 4 lb
　(2 kg), butterflied

salt and freshly ground pepper to taste

MARINADE
½ cup (4 fl oz/125 ml) olive oil

½ cup (4 fl oz/125 ml) Zinfandel or
　other dry red wine

6 cloves garlic, minced

1 tablespoon Dijon mustard

1½ tablespoons minced fresh
　rosemary

When a barbecue calls for an impressive centerpiece, a butter-flied leg of lamb is a popular choice. Ask your butcher to bone the leg for you, then marinate it briefly in a mixture of Zinfandel, mustard, and rosemary. To drink? Zinfandel, of course.

1. Trim all visible fat from the lamb, then trim away the thin external membrane.

2. To make the marinade, in a bowl, whisk together the olive oil, wine, garlic, mustard, and rosemary. Put the lamb in a shallow nonaluminum container large enough to hold it comfortably. Add the marinade and turn the lamb to coat both sides with the marinade. Cover and refrigerate for 4 hours, turning the lamb in the marinade once or twice during that time.

3. Prepare a medium-hot fire in a grill with a cover.

4. Meanwhile, bring the lamb to room temperature. When the coals are ready, put half of them on either side of the grill pan. Make a drip pan from heavy-duty aluminum foil and position it between the coals.

5. Remove the lamb from the marinade and season well with salt and pepper. Preheat the grill rack. Put the lamb on the rack directly over the drip pan, external side down. Cover the grill, leaving the vents partially open, and cook until an instant-read thermometer inserted in the thickest part of the leg registers 125°F (52°C) for medium-rare. The cooking time will depend on the heat of your fire and the size of the lamb leg, but a 4-lb (2-kg) butterflied leg should take 35–40 minutes. Transfer to a cutting board, cover loosely with aluminum foil, and let rest for 15 minutes before carving.

6. Carve the lamb against the grain and arrange on a warmed platter. Serve immediately.

SERVES 8–10

NUTRITIONAL ANALYSIS PER SERVING
Calories 345 (Kilojoules 1,449); Protein 43 g; Carbohydrates 0 g; Total Fat 18 g;
Saturated Fat 5 g; Cholesterol 135 mg; Sodium 123 mg; Dietary Fiber 0 g

Grilled Halibut with Salsa Verde

SALSA VERDE

¾ cup (1 oz/30 g) minced fresh
parsley

⅔ cup (5 fl oz/160 ml) extra-virgin
olive oil

6 anchovy fillets, finely minced

2 tablespoons chopped capers

1 large clove garlic, minced

1 tablespoon fresh lemon juice

½ cup (1 oz/30 g) soft fresh bread
crumbs

salt and freshly ground pepper to taste

6 halibut steaks or fillets, 6–8 oz
(185–250 g) each

olive oil

salt and freshly ground pepper to taste

Made of minced parsley and olive oil and enlivened with capers, anchovies, and garlic, Italian salsa verde (green sauce) is a classic partner for boiled meats and seafood. But its zesty nature enhances simple grilled fish, too, earning it a place on California tables.

1. Prepare a medium-hot fire in a grill.

2. To make the salsa verde, in a bowl, stir together the parsley, olive oil, anchovies, capers, garlic, and lemon juice. Stir in the bread crumbs. Season with salt and pepper. You should have 1 generous cup (8 fl oz/250 ml).

3. Measure the thickness of the fish steaks or fillets. Then coat the fish lightly on both sides with olive oil and season with salt and pepper.

4. When the coals are ready, spread them out to cover an area slightly larger than the surface area required for cooking the fish. Put the grill rack in place and let it preheat to prevent the fish from sticking.

5. Place the fish on the rack directly over the coals. You may cover the grill or not, as you prefer. Covering the grill, with the vents open, will cause the fish to cook faster and impart a smokier taste. If the fish is less than 1 inch (2.5 cm) thick, it's a good idea to cook it uncovered to prevent overcooking. Plan on 8–10 minutes of cooking time for each inch (2.5 cm) of thickness, and turn the fish halfway through.

6. Transfer the fish to warmed individual plates and put a generous spoonful of the salsa verde on top or alongside. Serve immediately.

SERVES 6

NUTRITIONAL ANALYSIS PER SERVING
Calories 437 (Kilojoules 1,835); Protein 35 g; Carbohydrates 3 g; Total Fat 32 g;
Saturated Fat 5 g; Cholesterol 54 mg; Sodium 385 mg; Dietary Fiber 0 g

Grilled Pork with Grilled Plum Sauce

A flavored brine restores the moisture and taste that today's lean pork used to have naturally. Many California chefs use the technique on all cuts of pork, but the extra-lean pork tenderloins particularly benefit.

1. To make the brine, in a saucepan, combine the water, salt, honey, thyme, garlic, and red pepper flakes. Bring to a boil over high heat, stirring to dissolve the salt and honey. Remove from the heat and let cool completely. Transfer the brine to a nonaluminum container, then add the pork, making sure it is completely submerged. Cover and refrigerate for 8–12 hours. Bring the pork to room temperature just before grilling.

2. Prepare a medium-hot fire in a grill with a cover. When the coals are ready, remove the pork from the brine and pat dry. Rub all over with the 1 tablespoon olive oil. Do not season the pork further. Coat the plum quarters with the remaining 2 teaspoons olive oil.

3. Put the pork on the grill rack directly over the coals. Cover the grill, keeping the grill vents open, and cook, turning once, until an instant-read thermometer inserted into the thickest part of the tenderloin registers 145°F (63°C), about 15 minutes. Transfer to a platter and let rest for 10 minutes before carving.

4. While the pork is resting, grill the plums on both cut sides until they are soft but not mushy, about 5 minutes on each side. Transfer to a cutting board and chop finely. In a small saucepan over medium heat, combine the plums, butter, and the 1 tablespoon sugar and cook, stirring, just until the butter melts and the sugar is dissolved. Taste and add more sugar, if needed. Reduce the heat to low and keep warm.

5. Slice the pork about ½ inch (12 mm) thick. Arrange on warmed individual plates. Spoon some of the plum sauce alongside. Serve immediately.

SERVES 4

NUTRITIONAL ANALYSIS PER SERVING
Calories 352 (Kilojoules 1,478); Protein 35 g; Carbohydrates 16 g; Total Fat 16 g;
Saturated Fat 6 g; Cholesterol 116 mg; Sodium 443 mg; Dietary Fiber 2 g

BRINE

8 cups (64 fl oz/2 l) water

½ cup (4 oz/125 g) kosher salt

¼ cup (3 fl oz/90 ml) honey

6–8 fresh thyme sprigs

2 cloves garlic, halved

1 teaspoon red pepper flakes

2 pork tenderloins, about ¾ lb (375 g) each

1 tablespoon plus 2 teaspoons olive oil

4 large Santa Rosa plums, quartered and pitted

1 tablespoon unsalted butter

1 tablespoon sugar, or to taste

Ahi Tuna with Red Pepper–Almond Sauce

SAUCE

⅓ cup (2 oz/60 g) whole unskinned
   almonds

1 large red bell pepper (capsicum)

1 large clove garlic

large pinch of salt, plus salt to taste

1 egg yolk

few drops warm water

⅔ cup (5 fl oz/160 ml) olive oil

2 teaspoons red wine vinegar,
   or to taste

cayenne pepper to taste

6 ahi tuna steaks, each ½ lb (250 g)
   and 1 inch (2.5 cm) thick, trimmed
   of skin and any dark parts

salt and freshly ground black pepper
   to taste

2 tablespoons olive oil

This dish is easiest to execute on a gas stove top that responds immediately when you reduce the flame. To achieve good results on an electric stove, set two burners to high heat for the searing and two to medium heat to finish.

1. To make the sauce, preheat the oven to 350°F (180°C). Spread the almonds on a baking sheet and toast until fragrant and lightly colored, about 15 minutes. Remove from the oven, let cool, and then grind in a food processor until medium-fine. Set aside.

2. Turn the oven to broil (grill). Cut the bell pepper in half lengthwise and remove the stem, seeds, and ribs. Place, cut sides down, on a baking sheet. Broil (grill) until the skin blackens and blisters. Remove from the broiler (griller), drape with aluminum foil, and let cool for 10 minutes, then peel away the skin. Purée the bell pepper in the food processor until smooth.

3. Mince the garlic to a paste with the pinch of salt. Transfer to a small bowl and whisk in the egg yolk and warm water. Begin adding the oil, drop by drop, whisking constantly to form an emulsion. Once the emulsion forms, you can add the oil in a thin stream. Whisk in the 2 teaspoons vinegar, the nuts, and the pepper purée. Season with salt and cayenne pepper, then taste and add more vinegar if desired. Cover and refrigerate until needed.

4. Pat the tuna dry and season with salt and black pepper. Set two large, heavy frying pans over high heat. When very hot, add 1 tablespoon of the oil to each pan and tilt to coat. When the oil is very hot, put 3 tuna steaks in each pan. Cook for 1 minute, then reduce the heat to medium and cook for 1 minute more. Turn the steaks over and cook until done to your taste, about 2 minutes for rare, 3 minutes for medium, and 4 minutes for medium-well.

5. Transfer to warmed individual plates. Spoon some of the sauce alongside each steak and serve immediately.

SERVES 6

NUTRITIONAL ANALYSIS PER SERVING
Calories 540 (Kilojoules 2,268); Protein 50 g; Carbohydrates 3 g; Total Fat 36 g;
Saturated Fat 5 g; Cholesterol 126 mg; Sodium 108 mg; Dietary Fiber 1 g

California
Wine

Relative to the seven-thousand-year history of wine making, California's experience with wine is brief. Father Junipero Serra planted the first wine grapes in the future state in 1769 at Mission San Diego. Three years later, the vines produced California's first vintage.

Today, the state's more than seven hundred wineries produce three out of every four bottles consumed in the United States. What progress for an industry that was virtually shut down during the fourteen years of Prohibition! And as a testament to the international renown of California wines, exports are growing steadily, claiming about 8 percent of production.

Although the Napa Valley is world famous, wine grapes are grown in many California counties, from San Diego to near the Oregon border. The state's five wine regions—north coast, central coast, south coast, Central Valley, and Sierra foothills—encompass a huge range of soils and microclimates, allowing California to produce everything from delicate French-inspired Pinot Noirs to massive, intense, only-in-California Zinfandels.

To consider them separately:

North Coast This area includes the counties of Napa, Sonoma, Lake, and Mendocino, all well known for high-quality wine. Wineries here work with mostly high-value grapes such as Cabernet Sauvignon, Pinot Noir, Merlot, Chardonnay, and Sauvignon Blanc.

Central Coast Stretching from San Francisco to Santa Barbara, this large area includes exceptional Cabernet Sauvignons from the Santa Cruz Mountains. The cooler regions of San Luis Obispo and Santa Barbara yield elegant Pinot Noirs and Chardonnays.

South Coast A developing wine region, this moderately warm stretch has plantings of Chardonnay, Zinfandel, and the historic Mission grape.

Central Valley Wineries seeking to make moderately priced wines often use Central Valley grapes. The region's high temperatures and fertile soil produce high yields.

Sierra Foothills The handful of wineries in former gold rush country make Zinfandels of renown.

Although most California wineries initially focused on the prestigious French wine grapes of Burgundy and Bordeaux, many are branching out. Today, California Zinfandel, believed to have southern Italian origins, has a huge following. Other wineries are looking to Italy for inspiration and planting Sangiovese, Nebbiolo, Pinot Grigio, and Tocai Friulano. A third contingent favors the grapes of France's Rhône region, such as Syrah, Marsanne, and Mourvèdre. Whatever else can be said about the California wine industry, its wine makers are not afraid to experiment.

Grapes growing on the vine in Napa County (opposite). The fruit of the wine maker's labor (below).

Fennel Sausage with Broccoli Rabe

2 lb (1 kg) broccoli rabe

4 hot or mild Italian fennel sausages, about 5 oz (155 g) each

2 teaspoons olive oil, plus more if needed

4 large cloves garlic, minced

¼ teaspoon red pepper flakes, or to taste

salt to taste

½ cup (2 oz/60 g) grated pecorino cheese

A favorite family dish in southern Italy, sausage with broccoli rabe also appears on contemporary California menus because so many local chefs feel a kinship with their Italian counterparts. In recent years, even grocery stores have begun carrying the slightly bitter green that was once hard to find outside Italian-American communities.

1. Trim away any woody stems from the broccoli rabe. Slit any remaining stems that are thicker than a pencil. Bring a large saucepan three-fourths full of salted water to a boil over high heat. Add the broccoli rabe and boil until the stems are tender, 3–4 minutes. Drain and rinse under cold running water to stop the cooking. Drain again, squeeze to remove any excess moisture, and then chop coarsely.

2. Preheat the oven to low.

3. Prick the sausages in several places. In a large frying pan over medium heat, warm the 2 teaspoons olive oil. Add the sausages and cook, turning once, until well browned and firm, about 20 minutes. Transfer to a platter and keep warm in the oven.

4. Pour off the rendered fat in the frying pan and measure it. Return 3 tablespoons of the fat to the pan, adding olive oil if necessary. Return the frying pan to medium-low heat and add the garlic and red pepper flakes. Sauté, stirring, until the garlic is fragrant and lightly colored, about 1 minute. Add the chopped broccoli rabe and season with salt. Stir to coat with the seasonings. Cook until the broccoli rabe is hot throughout, about 3 minutes.

5. Slice the sausages. Divide the broccoli rabe and sausages evenly among warmed individual plates. Top with the cheese, again dividing evenly. Serve immediately.

SERVES 4

NUTRITIONAL ANALYSIS PER SERVING
Calories 659 (Kilojoules 2,768); Protein 30 g; Carbohydrates 9 g; Total Fat 57 g; Saturated Fat 21 g; Cholesterol 127 mg; Sodium 1,277 mg; Dietary Fiber 0 g

Five-Spice Chicken with Cucumber Salad

1 chicken, 3½–4 lb (1.75–2 kg)

6 cloves garlic

4 teaspoons sugar

¼ cup (2 fl oz/60 ml) soy sauce

¼ cup (2 fl oz/60 ml) Thai or
   Vietnamese fish sauce

½ teaspoon five-spice powder

freshly ground pepper to taste

fresh cilantro (fresh coriander) sprigs

CUCUMBER SALAD

½ English (hothouse) cucumber,
   halved lengthwise, seeded, and
   thinly sliced

¼ red (Spanish) onion, thinly sliced

2 tablespoons chopped fresh cilantro
   (fresh coriander)

½ recipe (about ¼ cup/2 fl oz/60 ml)
   Vietnamese dipping sauce
   (page 84)

2 tablespoons coarsely chopped
   roasted peanuts

Five-spice chicken seemed exotic to me years ago, but the flavors are familiar now. Thanks to California's enthusias[m] for Vietnamese dishes such as this one, fish sauce and fi[ve]-spice powder are now supermarket staples.

1. Cut the chicken into 6 pieces: 2 leg-thigh pieces, 2 breast halves, and 2 wings. Remove the wing tips and save with the back for stock.

2. Combine the garlic and sugar in a mortar and pound to a paste. Transfer to a small bowl and whisk in the soy sauce, fish sauce, five-spice powder, and pepper. Put the chicken in a shallow dish, add the marinade, and turn the pieces to coat. Cover and refrigerate for 2 hours, turning the pieces several times. Bring to room temperature before grilling.

3. Prepare a medium-hot fire in a grill with a cover. When the coals are ready, divide them into 2 piles and arrange on either side of the grill. Put the grill rack in place and preheat it.

4. Remove the chicken from the marinade, reserving the marinade, and place the chicken, skin side down, in the center of the rack, not directly over the coals. Cover the grill, leaving the vents open. Cook until the skin side is richly browned, 10–12 minutes. Turn, baste with the marinade, and cover the grill. Cook, basting once or twice, until the juices run clear when the meat is pierced, 10–15 minutes longer. Do not baste during the final 5 minutes of cooking.

5. While the chicken cooks, make the cucumber salad: In a bowl, combine the cucumber, red onion, and chopped cilantro. Add the dipping sauce and toss well. Transfer to a serving bowl and top with the peanuts.

6. Chop the breast pieces and leg-thigh pieces in half. Transfer the chicken to a platter and garnish with cilantro sprigs. Serve with the salad.

SERVES 4

NUTRITIONAL ANALYSIS PER SERVING
Calories 562 (Kilojoules 2,360); Protein 57 g; Carbohydrates 15 g; Total Fat 30 g;
Saturated Fat 8 g; Cholesterol 165 mg; Sodium 1,330 mg; Dietary Fiber 2 g

Poached Halibut in Saffron Broth

Its firm, snowy white flesh makes Pacific halibut a California favorite for grilling, baking, or poaching.

1. Peel the shrimp and devein if desired. Put the shells in a saucepan with the water, wine, celery, carrot, onion, parsley sprigs, and bay leaf. Place over medium heat, bring to a simmer, and then adjust the heat to maintain a gentle simmer. Cook for 20 minutes, then strain the broth.

2. Meanwhile, make the aioli: In a small bowl, whisk the egg yolks until blended. Add the olive oil drop by drop, whisking constantly to make an emulsion. When the emulsion has formed, you can add the oil in a thin stream. Whisk in the garlic. Season with salt, cover, and refrigerate.

3. Transfer ¼ cup (2 fl oz/60 ml) of the hot broth to a bowl, add the saffron, and set aside. Pour 1½ cups (12 fl oz/375 ml) of the broth into a frying pan large enough to hold the fish fillets in a single layer. Season with salt and pepper. Reserve the remaining broth for another use. Bring the broth in the frying pan to a simmer over medium heat. Add the fish, cover, and adjust the heat to maintain a gentle simmer. Cook until the fish is opaque throughout and just flakes, about 8 minutes; the timing will depend upon the thickness. Using a slotted spatula, transfer the fish to warmed soup bowls and keep warm in a low oven. Add the shrimp to the broth, cover, and simmer until they turn white, 1–2 minutes. Using a slotted spoon, transfer the shrimp to the bowls.

4. Add the saffron-flavored broth to the broth in the frying pan. Whisk about ½ cup (4 fl oz/125 ml) of the hot broth into the aioli to warm it, then pour the thinned aioli into the frying pan. Cook over medium-low heat, stirring constantly with a wooden spoon, until the broth thickens slightly. Do not allow it to boil. Taste for salt.

5. Pour some of the thickened broth into each bowl. (You may not need it all.) Garnish with the minced parsley and serve immediately.

SERVES 4

NUTRITIONAL ANALYSIS PER SERVING
Calories 518 (Kilojoules 2,176); Protein 47 g; Carbohydrates 3 g; Total Fat 34 g; Saturated Fat 5 g; Cholesterol 234 mg; Sodium 175 mg; Dietary Fiber 1 g

24 medium-sized shrimp (prawns) in the shell

2½ cups (20 fl oz/625 ml) water

1 cup (8 fl oz/250 ml) dry white wine

1 small celery stalk, chopped

1 small carrot, peeled and chopped

½ yellow onion, halved

4 fresh flat-leaf (Italian) parsley sprigs, plus 1 tablespoon minced

1 bay leaf

¼ teaspoon saffron threads

salt and freshly ground pepper to taste

4 halibut or sea bass fillets, about 6 oz (185 g) each

AIOLI
2 egg yolks, at room temperature

½ cup (4 fl oz/125 ml) olive oil

1 large clove garlic, minced to a paste with a pinch of salt

salt to taste

Crisp Salmon with Warm Potato Salad

POTATO SALAD

1 tablespoon white wine vinegar

1½ teaspoons Dijon mustard

3 tablespoons olive oil

⅓ cup (1 oz/30 g) minced green
(spring) onion, white and pale
green parts only

1 tablespoon chopped capers

2 teaspoons chopped fresh tarragon

salt and freshly ground pepper to taste

1 lb (500 g) small boiling potatoes,
unpeeled, quartered

3 teaspoons olive oil

6 skinless salmon fillets, ½ lb (250 g)
each

salt and freshly ground pepper to taste

½ lb (250 g) watercress, thick stems
removed

6 lemon wedges

Searing fish in a hot frying pan to produce a crisp, browned surface is a popular technique among California chefs. To prevent the fillets from overbrowning before they are done, chefs finish the cooking in a moderate oven. The method works best, I find, with a fatty fish such as our Pacific king salmon.

1. To make the potato salad, in a small bowl, whisk together the vinegar and mustard. Gradually whisk in the olive oil to make an emulsion. Whisk in the green onion, capers, and tarragon. Season generously with salt and pepper.

2. In a saucepan over high heat, combine the potatoes with salted water to cover. Bring to a boil, adjust the heat to maintain a gentle simmer, and cook, checking often, until just tender when pierced, about 10 minutes. Drain thoroughly, then transfer to a large bowl and add the dressing. Toss to coat evenly. Let stand until warm, tossing occasionally so the dressing penetrates the potatoes evenly.

3. Meanwhile, preheat the oven to 375°F (190°C). Heat 2 large oven-proof frying pans over medium-high heat until hot. Add 1½ teaspoons of the oil to each pan, swirl to coat, and heat until the oil is almost smoking.

4. Season the salmon fillets on both sides with salt and pepper, then immediately put them in the pans, flat side (skin side) up. Cook until golden brown and crusty without moving the salmon, 1–2 minutes; lift a fillet slightly to check the progress. When browned, turn the fillets carefully and transfer the pans to the oven. Bake uncovered until the fillets are just opaque throughout, about 8 minutes. Transfer the fillets to paper towels briefly to drain any fat, then to individual plates.

5. Add the watercress to the potatoes and toss to coat with the dressing. Taste and adjust the seasonings. Divide the salad evenly among the plates. Garnish each portion with a lemon wedge and serve immediately.

SERVES 6

NUTRITIONAL ANALYSIS PER SERVING
Calories 567 (Kilojoules 2,381); Protein 48 g; Carbohydrates 16 g; Total Fat 34 g;
Saturated Fat 6 g; Cholesterol 134 mg; Sodium 249 mg; Dietary Fiber 2 g

Dungeness Crab Cakes with Cabbage Slaw

¼ cup (2 fl oz/60 ml) mayonnaise

2 teaspoons dry mustard

salt and cayenne pepper to taste

¼ cup (1½ oz/45 g) finely minced
celery

¼ cup (¾ oz/20 g) finely minced
green (spring) onion, white and
pale green parts only

1 lb (500 g) fresh-cooked Dungeness
crabmeat, picked over for shell
fragments

2 cups (4 oz/120 g) soft fresh bread
crumbs

4 teaspoons olive oil

4 teaspoons unsalted butter

4 lemon wedges

CABBAGE SLAW

¼ cup (2 fl oz/60 ml) buttermilk

¼ cup (2 fl oz/60 ml) mayonnaise

2 tablespoons minced fresh dill

1 clove garlic, minced

4 cups (12 oz/375 g) thinly sliced
Napa cabbage

1 cup (4 oz/125 g) grated carrot

¼ cup (¾ oz/20 g) minced green
(spring) onion

salt and freshly ground black pepper
to taste

fresh lemon juice to taste

Many East Coast cooks add a liberal dash of Old Bay seasoning to their blue-crab cakes, but California cooks using the local Dungeness take a lighter approach. These crab cakes have just enough mayonnaise to hold them together and just enough seasoning to heighten, not hide, the crab flavor.

1. To make the crab cakes, in a bowl, stir together the mayonnaise and mustard. Add a pinch each of salt and cayenne pepper. Stir in the celery and green onion, then gently fold in the crabmeat and 1 cup (2 oz/60 g) of the bread crumbs. Spread the remaining 1 cup (2 oz/60 g) bread crumbs on a sheet of waxed paper.

2. Shape the crab mixture into 8 patties, each 1 inch (2.5 cm) thick. They will only reluctantly hold together, but try not to overwork them. Coat them on both sides with the bread crumbs, then arrange on a baking sheet. Cover and refrigerate for 1 hour.

3. While the crab cakes are chilling, make the slaw: In a small bowl, whisk together the buttermilk, mayonnaise, dill, and garlic. In a large bowl, toss together the cabbage, carrot, and green onion. Add the dressing and salt and black pepper to taste and toss well. Taste and add as much lemon juice as desired.

4. Heat 2 large nonstick frying pans over medium heat. Put 2 teaspoons oil and 2 teaspoons butter in each pan. When the fat is hot, put 4 crab cakes in each pan. Cook until golden brown on the bottom, about 3 minutes. Turn and cook until the second side is well browned and the cakes are hot throughout, 3–4 minutes longer.

5. Transfer to individual plates and serve immediately with the lemon wedges and the slaw.

SERVES 4

NUTRITIONAL ANALYSIS PER SERVING
Calories 510 (Kilojoules 2,142); Protein 28 g; Carbohydrates 24 g; Total Fat 34 g;
Saturated Fat 7 g; Cholesterol 142 mg; Sodium 659 mg; Dietary Fiber 3 g

I t's a perfect winter lunch: a chunk of sourdough bread and butter, a glass of crisp California Chardonnay, and a heaping platter of cold cracked Dungeness crab. At seafood bars like the venerable Swan Oyster Depot in San Francisco, crab enthusiasts enjoy the sweet, firm meat of *Cancer magister* with Louis dressing or with olive oil and a spritz of lemon. In California's Chinatowns, chefs pull the crabs live from tanks and stir-fry them with salted black beans or with ginger and green (spring) onions.

The Dungeness crab has been fished commercially—and enthusi-astically—in California since gold rush days. Among the most beloved of California's many seafood species, the red-shelled crabs seduce diners with generous portions of snowy white meat in their claws and body. The whole crabs typically weigh 1½ to 3 pounds (750 g to 1.5 kg) and yield about a quarter of their weight in meat.

From central California north to the Oregon border, fishermen har-vest the crab in traps. To ensure future stocks, they keep only male crabs at least 6¼ inches (15.5 cm) wide. In Northern California, where

Dungeness **Crab**

these shellfish are most abundant, the commercial season runs from December 1 to July 15.

For home consumption, some shoppers buy crab already cooked. Others buy them live and boil them in water, white wine, aromatic veg-etables, and herbs. Then they set out crab crackers, whip up a dipping sauce, and sit down to a feast.

Pan-Roasted Duck with Dried-Cherry Sauce

4 boneless, skinless duck breast
   halves

salt and freshly ground pepper to taste

1 tablespoon olive oil

4 tablespoons (2 oz/60 g) unsalted
   butter

1 large shallot, minced

¾ cup (6 fl oz/180 ml) Port

⅓ cup (1½ oz/45 g) dried pitted
   cherries

2 cups (16 fl oz/500 ml) duck or
   chicken stock, boiled until reduced
   to 1 cup (8 fl oz/250 ml)

2 teaspoons cherry preserves
   or 1 teaspoon sugar

2 teaspoons balsamic vinegar

Roast duck is one of my favorite partners for California's esteemed Pinot Noirs. In this recipe, a dried-cherry sauce makes the food and wine marriage even better because so many Pinot Noirs have cherry nuances. If you must buy two ducks to get the four breasts required here, save the legs for braising and use the carcasses to make stock.

1. Preheat the oven to 375°F (190°C).

2. Season the duck breasts on both sides with salt and pepper. Heat a large ovenproof frying pan over high heat until hot. Add the olive oil and swirl to coat the pan. When the oil is hot, add the duck breasts, skinned side down. Reduce the heat to medium-high and cook until nicely browned, 1½–2 minutes. Turn and cook until the second side is lightly browned, 1½–2 minutes longer. Transfer the frying pan to the oven and roast until an instant-read thermometer inserted into the thickest part of the breast registers 125°F (52°C), about 5 minutes, or until done to your liking. Transfer the breasts to a platter and let rest while you make the sauce.

3. Pour off any fat remaining in the frying pan. Add 1 tablespoon of the butter and return to medium-low heat. When the butter melts, add the shallot and sauté until softened, about 2 minutes. Add the Port and cherries, raise the heat to high, and simmer until the pan is almost dry. Add the reduced stock, cherry preserves or sugar, balsamic vinegar, and any duck juices that have collected on the platter. Boil until the sauce is reduced to about ⅔ cup (5 fl oz/160 ml) and is almost syrupy. Remove from the heat and add the remaining 3 tablespoons butter. Swirl the pan until the butter melts.

4. Slice the duck breasts on the diagonal and transfer to warmed dinner plates. Top with the sauce, dividing it evenly. Serve immediately.

SERVES 4

NUTRITIONAL ANALYSIS PER SERVING
Calories 376 (Kilojoules 1,579); Protein 35 g; Carbohydrates 21 g; Total Fat 16 g;
Saturated Fat 8 g; Cholesterol 210 mg; Sodium 686 mg; Dietary Fiber 0 g

Grilled Hanger Steaks with Anchovy Butter

ANCHOVY BUTTER

1 teaspoon peppercorns

2 large cloves garlic, sliced

large pinch of salt

12 anchovy fillets in olive oil, drained

6 tablespoons unsalted butter, softened

2 hanger steaks, about 1¾ lb (875 g) each

2 tablespoons extra-virgin olive oil

salt and freshly ground pepper to taste

watercress sprigs

In the past, most California butchers ground hanger steak, but this cut has become so popular that some shops now sell it whole. A long, thick muscle, the hanger steak lies behind the cow's last rib. In summer, it's one of my favorite meats to grill over a charcoal fire. Flank steak could also be used.

1. Prepare a medium-hot charcoal fire in a grill with a cover.

2. To make the anchovy butter, in a mortar, pound the peppercorns until coarsely ground. Add the garlic and salt and pound to a rough paste. Add the anchovies and pound to a rough paste. Add the butter and pound until the mixture is smooth. Taste and adjust the seasonings. Set aside.

3. Trim the steaks of all visible fat. Cut out the silvery membrane between the two lobes of each steak. Tie the lobes of each steak together at 2-inch (5-cm) intervals with kitchen string. Rub all over with the oil.

4. When the fire is ready, divide the coals into two piles and arrange on either side of the grate. Put the grill rack in place and preheat it. Season the steaks with salt and pepper. Place the steaks in the center of the rack, not directly over the coals. Cover the grill, leaving the top and bottom vents open. Cook until the meat is nicely browned on the bottom, 6–7 minutes. Turn, re-cover, and continue to cook for about 5 minutes more for rare (an internal temperature of 120°F/49°C) or 6–7 minutes for medium-rare (130°F/54°C). Hanger steak should not be cooked beyond medium-rare. Transfer the steaks to a platter and let rest for 5 minutes.

5. Transfer the steaks to a cutting board, remove the strings, and slice about ½ inch (12 mm) thick. Arrange the slices on a large, warmed platter and immediately top with the anchovy butter, spreading it evenly over the meat with a spatula. It will melt quickly. If there are meat juices on the platter that the meat rested on, spoon those over the meat, too. Garnish the platter with watercress and serve immediately.

SERVES 6

NUTRITIONAL ANALYSIS PER SERVING
Calories 599 (Kilojoules 2,516); Protein 54 g; Carbohydrates 1 g; Total Fat 41 g; Saturated Fat 18 g; Cholesterol 167 mg; Sodium 482 mg; Dietary Fiber 0 g

Lamb with White Beans and Gremolata

Because much of California has a Mediterranean climate, the food of southern France and of Italy seems at home in the state's kitchens. This dish borrows from both countries.

1. Pick over the beans to remove any stones and rinse well. Place in a bowl with water to cover by about 2 inches (5 cm) and let soak overnight.

2. The next day, heat a large, heavy pot over medium-high heat. Add 1 tablespoon of the oil and swirl to coat the bottom. When the oil is hot, add the lamb shanks and season with salt and pepper. Reduce the heat to medium and brown the shanks, turning as necessary, about 20 minutes. Transfer to a plate and pour off the fat in the pot. Return the pot to medium heat and add the remaining 2 tablespoons oil. Add the onion and herbes de Provence and sauté until soft, about 8 minutes. Add the garlic and sauté for 1–2 minutes until fragrant.

3. Meanwhile, halve the tomatoes lengthwise. Using a fingertip, scoop out and discard the seeds. Grate the tomato pulp on the large holes of a grater/shredder, discarding the skin. Add the tomatoes to the pot and season with salt and pepper. Cook, stirring, for 5 minutes. Return the lamb shanks to the pot and add the orange zest and 1 cup (8 fl oz/250 ml) of the water. Bring to a gentle simmer, cover, and cook for 1 hour.

4. Drain the beans and add them to the pot along with the remaining 2 cups (16 fl oz/500 ml) water. Bring to a simmer, cover, and cook until the shanks and beans are tender, about 1½ hours. Let rest for 30 minutes, then spoon off as much fat as possible. Taste and adjust the seasonings. Reheat over medium-low heat. Meanwhile, make the gremolata: In a small bowl, combine the parsley, lemon zest, and garlic.

5. Divide the shanks and beans among warmed individual bowls. Top each portion with some of the gremolata. Serve immediately.

SERVES 4

2 cups (14 oz/440 g) dried cannellini beans or other large white beans

3 tablespoons olive oil

4 small lamb shanks, about 2¾ lb (1.4 kg) total weight

salt and freshly ground pepper to taste

3 cups (12 oz/375 g) chopped yellow onion

1 tablespoon dried herbes de Provence

3 cloves garlic, minced

1 lb (500 g) plum (Roma) tomatoes

2 orange zest strips

3 cups (24 fl oz/750 ml) water

GREMOLATA

2 tablespoons minced fresh flat-leaf (Italian) parsley

1 teaspoon grated lemon zest

1 small clove garlic, finely minced

NUTRITIONAL ANALYSIS PER SERVING
Calories 894 (Kilojoules 3,755); Protein 74 g; Carbohydrates 74 g; Total Fat 34 g;
Saturated Fat 11 g; Cholesterol 165 mg; Sodium 149 mg; Dietary Fiber 12 g

Swordfish Paillards with Green Olive Relish

RELISH

½ cup (2 oz/60 g) walnuts

1 large red bell pepper (capsicum)

½ cup (2½ oz/75 g) rinsed, pitted, and finely chopped green olives such as French Picholine

¼ cup (⅓ oz/10 g) finely chopped fresh mint

6 tablespoons (3 fl oz/90 ml) extra-virgin olive oil

2 tablespoons fresh lemon juice

2 cloves garlic, minced

salt and freshly ground pepper to taste

6 swordfish steaks, about 6 oz (185 g) each and a scant ½ inch (12 mm) thick

2 tablespoons extra-virgin olive oil

salt and freshly ground pepper to taste

Paillard is the French term for a thin slice of boneless meat, but some chefs, with poetic license, use the same word for thinly sliced fish. For the relish, choose lightly brined, unseasoned green olives that don't taste too sharp or salty; avoid those packed in vinegar.

1. To make the relish, preheat the oven to 350°F (180°C). Spread the walnuts on a baking sheet and toast in the oven until lightly colored and fragrant, about 15 minutes. Transfer to a cutting board, let cool, then chop finely.

2. Turn the oven to broil (grill). Cut the bell pepper in half lengthwise and remove the stem, seeds, and ribs. Place, cut sides down, on a baking sheet. Broil (grill) until the skin blackens and blisters. Remove from the broiler (griller), leaving the broiler on. Drape the pepper loosely with aluminum foil and let cool for 10 minutes, then peel away the skin. Finely chop half of the pepper. Reserve the other half for another use.

3. In a bowl, combine the walnuts, chopped bell pepper, olives, mint, olive oil, lemon juice, and garlic. Season with salt and pepper. Set aside until serving.

4. Position the broiler rack about 8 inches (20 cm) from the heat source. Oil the swordfish on both sides with the olive oil. Arrange the fish on a heavy baking sheet. Season with salt and pepper.

5. Broil (grill) the fish until it is opaque throughout and just flakes, about 5 minutes. Transfer to individual plates and top with the olive relish, dividing it evenly. Serve immediately.

SERVES 6

NUTRITIONAL ANALYSIS PER SERVING
Calories 425 (Kilojoules 1,785); Protein 32 g; Carbohydrates 4 g; Total Fat 32 g; Saturated Fat 5 g; Cholesterol 59 mg; Sodium 422 mg; Dietary Fiber 1 g

Seared Beef and Asian Greens

1 lb (500 g) well-trimmed beef sirloin or London broil

2 tablespoons Thai or Vietnamese fish sauce

2 tablespoons peanut oil

1 tablespoon soy sauce

½ teaspoon Asian sesame oil

2 large cloves garlic, minced

several grinds of pepper

½ lb (250 g) Asian stir-fry greens such as baby mustard and tat-soi

24 fresh Asian basil leaves, torn into small pieces

½ red (Spanish) onion, thinly sliced

salt to taste

DRESSING

3 tablespoons peanut oil

2 tablespoons fresh lime juice

1 large shallot, minced

1 serrano chile, seeded and minced

½ teaspoon sugar

Many California markets now carry a blend of pungent baby greens suitable for stir-frying or for warm salads such as this one. Here, thin strips of lean beef are marinated with Asian seasonings, then quickly seared and tossed with the leafy greens. If you can't find Asian stir-fry greens, substitute a mixture of spinach and watercress.

1. Place the meat in the freezer for about 30 minutes to make it easier to slice. Then thinly slice against the grain into strips about 2 inches (5 cm) long and 1 inch (2.5 cm) wide and place in a large bowl. Add the fish sauce, 1 tablespoon of the peanut oil, soy sauce, sesame oil, garlic, and pepper and toss to coat evenly. Let stand for 30 minutes at room temperature.

2. To make the dressing, in a small bowl, whisk together the peanut oil, lime juice, shallot, chile, and sugar. Let stand for 30 minutes to allow the shallot flavor to mellow.

3. Just before you are ready to cook the meat, put the stir-fry greens, basil, and red onion in a large serving bowl. Add the dressing and toss to coat evenly.

4. Heat a 12-inch (30-cm) frying pan over high heat. When the pan is hot, add the remaining 1 tablespoon peanut oil and swirl to coat the pan. When the oil is very hot, add the meat and stir and toss until it loses most of its red color, 30–45 seconds; the meat should still be rare.

5. Add the contents of the pan to the bowl with the greens and toss well. Season with salt and pepper and serve immediately.

SERVES 4

NUTRITIONAL ANALYSIS PER SERVING
Calories 357 (Kilojoules 1,499); Protein 28 g; Carbohydrates 9 g; Total Fat 23 g; Saturated Fat 5 g; Cholesterol 69 mg; Sodium 638 mg; Dietary Fiber 1 g

Grilled Salmon with Cucumber Raita

RAITA

½ English (hothouse) cucumber

¼ teaspoon salt, plus salt to taste

¼ teaspoon cumin seeds

1 cup (8 oz/250 g) plain whole-milk
    yogurt

1 large plum (Roma) tomato, quartered
    lengthwise, seeded, and thinly
    sliced crosswise

2 teaspoons finely chopped fresh mint

1 serrano chile, seeded and finely
    minced

⅛ teaspoon cayenne pepper

4 salmon fillets with skin intact,
    about 6 oz (185 g) each

4 teaspoons olive oil

salt and freshly ground black pepper
    to taste

The incessant borrowing that characterizes the California kitchen extends to the Indian repertoire, too. As California cooks have discovered, India's yogurt salads—known collectively as raitas—are delicious with grilled fish and meats. Here, a cucumber-and-tomato raita is paired with grilled salmon.

1. To make the raita, peel the cucumber, halve lengthwise, and scrape out any seeds. Shred on the large holes of a grater/shredder. Sprinkle with the ¼ teaspoon salt, then place in a sieve to drain for 30 minutes.

2. Meanwhile, in a small frying pan over medium heat, toast the cumin seeds until fragrant and lightly colored, about 3 minutes. Transfer to a mortar or spice grinder and grind to a powder. In a bowl, combine the yogurt, tomato, mint, chile, cayenne, and ground cumin. Stir to mix. Add the cucumber just before serving. Season with salt.

3. While the cucumber is draining, prepare a medium-hot fire in a grill with a cover.

4. When the fire is ready, divide the coals into two piles and arrange on either side of the grate. Put the grill rack in place and preheat it. Coat each salmon fillet with 1 teaspoon olive oil and season with salt and black pepper. Place the fillets, skin side down, in the center of the grill rack, not directly over the coals. Cover the grill, leaving the top and bottom vents open. Cook until the fish is just opaque throughout, 6–8 minutes.

5. Slip a long, offset spatula between the skin and flesh of the fillets and transfer the fillets to warmed individual plates, leaving the skin behind. Spoon some of the raita over the salmon. Pass the remaining raita at the table.

SERVES 4

NUTRITIONAL ANALYSIS PER SERVING
Calories 371 (Kilojoules 1,558); Protein 33 g; Carbohydrates 5 g; Total Fat 23 g;
Saturated Fat 5 g; Cholesterol 99 mg; Sodium 266 mg; Dietary Fiber 0 g

I n a state whose climate allows eating outdoors much of the year, it's hardly surprising that charcoal grilling has become something of an art form.

Not all California homes have backyards, but they might have terraces, patios, or decks to accommodate that favorite weekend festivity: the backyard barbecue. Increasingly, California homeowners are installing outdoor kitchens that range from the humble to the grand, with a brick oven for bread and pizza and a charcoal grill for everything else.

Indeed, in their wholehearted embrace of outdoor living, Californians will grill just about anything, including pizza. We grill burgers, steaks, sausages, and chicken, as does the rest of the country. But we also grill whole sides of salmon and whole butterflied legs of lamb. We put local oysters on the grill until they open, and the more adventuresome eaters among us love grilling fresh California anchovies and sardines.

We grill goat cheese in grape leaves and then grill the bread to spread it on. We grill vegetables from asparagus to zucchini (courgettes), including such unconventional candidates as fennel and radicchio. We

Charcoal **Grilling**

grill peaches, bananas, and plums. At my house, we even cook the Thanksgiving turkey over charcoal.

Thirty years ago, charcoal grills were uncommon in California restaurants, apart from steakhouses and a handful of fish restaurants. Today, few chefs planning to offer contemporary California fare would open a restaurant without one.

Fried Squid with Vietnamese Dipping Sauce

1 lb (500 g) squid

1 tablespoon Thai or Vietnamese
fish sauce

freshly ground pepper to taste

1 cup (4 oz/125 g) cornstarch
(cornflour)

vegetable oil for deep-frying

fresh cilantro (fresh coriander) or
Asian basil sprigs

DIPPING SAUCE
1 small fresh red chile, halved and
seeded

1 large clove garlic

2 tablespoons sugar

pulp from ½ lime, without any
membrane

¼ cup (2 fl oz/60 ml) Thai or
Vietnamese fish sauce

2 tablespoons fresh lime juice

¼ cup (2 fl oz/60 ml) water

When my husband and I want a fast, inexpensive but whole-some meal, we head for one of the many modest Vietnamese restaurants in the San Francisco Bay Area. We like the fresh, healthful nature of the cooking; even fried foods, such as this dish, seem light.

1. To clean each squid, pull the head from the body. Cut off the tentacles and discard the head. Press the base of the tentacles to force out the "beak," and reserve the tentacles. With your finger, pull out any interior matter from the body, including the quill-like cartilage, then peel off the mottled skin that covers the outside. Cut the body crosswise into rings ½ inch (12 mm) wide. In a bowl, combine the squid rings and tentacles, fish sauce, and several grinds of pepper. Let marinate at room tempera-ture for 30 minutes.

2. Meanwhile, make the dipping sauce: In a small food processor, combine the chile, garlic, and sugar and process until finely chopped. Add the lime pulp and process again. Add the fish sauce and lime juice and process to mix. Transfer to a bowl and stir in the water. Taste and adjust the seasonings. (Alternatively, pound the ingredients together in a mortar, and stir in the water.) Divide between small individual bowls.

3. Drain the squid. Place in a bowl, add the cornstarch, and toss to coat. Transfer to a large sieve and shake off the excess.

4. In a saucepan, pour in vegetable oil to a depth of 2–3 inches (5–7.5 cm) and heat to 370°F (187°C) on a deep-frying thermometer. Working in 3 or 4 batches, add the squid and fry until golden, about 1 minute. Using a wire-mesh skimmer, transfer to a double thickness of paper towels to drain.

5. Line salad plates with white paper cocktail napkins. Divide the squid among the plates. Garnish with cilantro or Asian basil and serve immedi-ately, accompanied with the dipping sauce.

SERVES 2

NUTRITIONAL ANALYSIS PER SERVING
Calories 670 (Kilojoules 2,814); Protein 34 g; Carbohydrates 56 g; Total Fat 34 g;
Saturated Fat 6 g; Cholesterol 412 mg; Sodium 1,570 mg; Dietary Fiber 0 g

FARMERS M
3-1³⁰ SUNDAYS 9-1

WELCOME TO
CASTROVILL
"ARTICHOKE CENTER OF THE WO

MOTELS-RESTAURANTS-SERV

Angele's PRODUC
83124 LUPINE AVE
INDIO, CA.

LB
¹⁰⁰

3 Vegetables, Grains & Beans

California's large number of "almost vegetarians" have no trouble shaping a satisfying diet from the wealth of produce, grains, and beans available to them. Every season offers temptations: grilled asparagus in spring (page 94), risotto with fresh corn in summer (page 98), fettuccine with mushrooms and truffle oil in the fall (page 114). Italy has had a powerful influence on the state's kitchens. In homes and in restaurants, pasta, pizza, focaccia, and risotto are embedded in the culinary culture. Today, Asian flavors are on the rise, with widespread acceptance for dishes such as sesame noodles (page 92), stir-fried Chinese long beans (page 88), and roasted eggplant with oyster sauce (page 104).

Chinese Long Beans with Sesame Seeds

1½ tablespoons sesame seeds

1 lb (500 g) Chinese long beans, trimmed and cut into 3–4-inch (7.5–10-cm) lengths

1½ tablespoons peanut oil

2 tablespoons peeled and finely minced fresh ginger

1 large clove garlic, minced

1 serrano chile, seeded and minced

salt to taste

1 teaspoon Asian sesame oil

⅓ cup (½ oz/15 g) chopped fresh cilantro (fresh coriander)

Often called yard-long beans—with some hyperbole—these slender green beans can easily reach half a yard (45 cm) in length. In Chinatown markets from Los Angeles to San Francisco, you will inevitably find them for sale arranged in neat skeins. They take well to strong seasonings.

1. In a small, dry frying pan over medium heat, toast the sesame seeds, stirring often, until fragrant and lightly colored, about 5 minutes. Pour onto a small plate.

2. Bring a large saucepan three-fourths full of salted water to a boil over high heat. Add the beans and cook until just tender, about 5 minutes. Drain in a sieve and rinse with cold running water to stop the cooking. Drain thoroughly, then pat dry.

3. Place a 12-inch (30-cm) frying pan over medium-high heat. When it is hot, add the peanut oil and swirl to coat the pan. When the oil is hot, add the ginger, garlic, and chile and cook, stirring constantly, for about 30 seconds to release the fragrance of the ginger and garlic. Add the green beans and salt and toss to coat with the seasonings. Cook until the beans are hot throughout. Stir in the sesame seeds, reserving a few for garnish. Remove from the heat and add the sesame oil and cilantro. Toss well.

4. Transfer the beans to a large warmed platter. Top with the reserved sesame seeds and serve immediately.

SERVES 4

NUTRITIONAL ANALYSIS PER SERVING
Calories 110 (Kilojoules 462); Protein 3 g; Carbohydrates 9 g; Total Fat 8 g;
Saturated Fat 1 g; Cholesterol 0 mg; Sodium 8 mg; Dietary Fiber 2 g

Spring Vegetable Ragout

2 lemons

2 large artichokes

2 lb (1 kg) fava (broad) beans, shelled

ice water as needed

¼ cup (2 fl oz/60 ml) extra-virgin
olive oil

10 small spring onions or boiling
onions, about 1½ inches (4 cm) in
diameter, stalks removed and
bulbs halved vertically

2 turnips, thickly peeled, cut into
6 or 8 wedges

18 baby carrots, peeled

1 large fennel bulb, trimmed, halved
lengthwise, and thinly sliced
crosswise

¼ cup (2 fl oz/60 ml) water,
plus 2 tablespoons, if needed

salt and freshly ground pepper to taste

¼ cup (⅓ oz/10 g) chopped fresh dill

California's best cooks relish the change of the seasons and eagerly anticipate vegetables, such as fava beans and spring onions, that don't stay around long. When those two are in the market together, I like to make a simple ragout.

1. Fill a bowl with cold water and add the juice of 1 lemon. Halve the remaining lemon. Pull back the outer leaves of each artichoke until they break at the base. Continue removing the leaves until you reach the pale green, tender inner leaves. Cut about 1 inch (2.5 cm) off the top of each artichoke and all but 1 inch (2.5 cm) of the stem. Rub the cut surfaces with the lemon halves. Peel the stem and the base of each artichoke, removing any dark green parts. Rub with the lemon halves. Halve each artichoke vertically. Scrape out the hairy choke and prickly leaves, then cut each half into 4 wedges. Squeeze the lemon halves over the arti-chokes, then transfer the artichoke pieces to the lemon water.

2. Bring a saucepan three-fourths full of water to a boil over high heat. Drop in the fava beans and boil for 30 seconds if small, or for up to 1 minute if large. Drain and immerse in ice water to stop the cooking. When cool, drain again. Pinch open the end of each bean opposite the end that con-nects it to the pod. The beans will slip easily from their thin skins.

3. In a large pot, warm the olive oil over medium heat. Add the onions and cook, stirring occasionally, until softened, about 5 minutes. Add the artichokes and stir to coat with the oil. Cover and cook gently for 10 min-utes. Add the turnips, carrots, fennel, and the ¼ cup (2 fl oz/60 ml) water and season generously with salt and pepper. Cover and cook until the vegetables are almost tender, 5–8 minutes. Add the fava beans and dill; if the mixture seems dry, add the 2 tablespoons water. Cover and cook until all the vegetables are tender, about 5 minutes longer. Taste and adjust the seasonings. Transfer to a warmed serving bowl and serve.

SERVES 6

NUTRITIONAL ANALYSIS PER SERVING
Calories 187 (Kilojoules 785); Protein 7 g; Carbohydrates 21 g; Total Fat 10 g;
Saturated Fat 1 g; Cholesterol 0 mg; Sodium 201 mg; Dietary Fiber 8 g

Sesame Noodles

2 tablespoons peanut oil

1 teaspoon red pepper flakes

2 large cloves garlic, minced

2 tablespoons peeled and minced
fresh ginger

3 tablespoons Asian sesame oil

2 tablespoons soy sauce

1½ tablespoons balsamic vinegar

1½ tablespoons sugar

2 teaspoons salt

1 lb (500 g) thin fresh Chinese egg
noodles

12 green (spring) onions, white and
pale green parts only, thinly sliced

2 tablespoons sesame seeds

⅓ cup (½ oz/15 g) coarsely chopped
fresh cilantro (fresh coriander)

These room-temperature noodles are an excellent party or potluck dish because you can—in fact, should—make them one to two hours ahead. Resting longer won't hurt them. Serve as a warm-weather dinner with room-temperature roast chicken or make them the centerpiece of a picnic lunch.

1. In a small frying pan over medium heat, warm the peanut oil. Add the red pepper flakes and cook, stirring, until the oil develops some red color and the pepper flakes are fragrant. Add the garlic and ginger and cook, stirring, until fragrant and slightly soft, about 1 minute. Remove from the heat.

2. In a small bowl, whisk together the sesame oil, soy sauce, balsamic vinegar, sugar, and salt. Whisk in the garlic-ginger mixture.

3. Bring a large pot three-fourths full of salted water to a boil over high heat. Add the noodles, stir well, and cook until al dente, 2–3 minutes. Drain and rinse under cold running water until cold. Drain thoroughly, then transfer to a large bowl. Add the sauce and toss to coat the noodles evenly. Add the green onions, reserving about 2 tablespoons for garnish. Toss to mix. Cover and let stand at room temperature for 1–2 hours, tossing occasionally so the noodles absorb the seasonings evenly.

4. Just before serving, toast the sesame seeds: In a small, dry frying pan over medium heat, toast the sesame seeds, stirring often, until fragrant and lightly colored, about 5 minutes. Pour onto a plate to cool.

5. Add the sesame seeds and cilantro to the noodles, reserving about 2 tablespoons of the cilantro for garnish. Transfer the noodles to a large platter. Garnish with the reserved green onions and cilantro and serve.

SERVES 4

NUTRITIONAL ANALYSIS PER SERVING
Calories 548 (Kilojoules 2,302); Protein 15 g; Carbohydrates 74 g; Total Fat 22 g;
Saturated Fat 3 g; Cholesterol 83 mg; Sodium 2,106 mg; Dietary Fiber 4 g

Grilled Asparagus with Parmesan

2 bunches asparagus, 2–2½ lb
  (1–1.25 kg) total weight

ice water as needed

2 tablespoons extra-virgin olive oil

kosher salt

¼ cup (1 oz/30 g) grated Parmesan
  cheese

My husband and I encountered grilled asparagus in a tapas bar in Valencia, Spain, years ago, and we have rarely cooked it another way since. Often I put just olive oil and kosher salt on the spears, but to dress them up, I might add a shower of Parmesan cheese.

1. Prepare a hot fire in a grill. If possible, position the grill rack so that the asparagus will be only about 3 inches (7.5 cm) from the coals.

2. Holding an asparagus spear at the stem end and in the middle, bend the spear gently. It will break naturally at the point at which it becomes tough. Discard the tough ends. Repeat with the remaining spears. You should have about 1¼ lb (625 g) trimmed spears.

3. Bring a wide, shallow saucepan three-fourths full of salted water to a boil over high heat. Add the asparagus and boil until they are just beginning to become tender, 2–4 minutes, depending on size; they should still be somewhat crisp. Drain and immerse in ice water to stop the cooking. When cool, drain well and pat dry in a kitchen towel.

4. Put the spears on a baking sheet with all the tips pointing in the same direction. Drizzle with the olive oil and sprinkle with kosher salt. Turn to coat evenly with the oil and salt.

5. Place the asparagus on the preheated grill rack directly over the coals in a single layer, all the tips pointing in the same direction. Take care to place them across the bars so they don't fall into the fire. Cook until they blister, 1–2 minutes, then carefully turn with tongs and grill on the other side until blistered, 1–2 minutes longer.

6. Transfer to a platter and sprinkle with the Parmesan cheese. Serve immediately.

SERVES 4

NUTRITIONAL ANALYSIS PER SERVING
Calories 133 (Kilojoules 559); Protein 9 g; Carbohydrates 8 g; Total Fat 9 g;
Saturated Fat 2 g; Cholesterol 5 mg; Sodium 118 mg; Dietary Fiber 2 g

Concerned about pesticide residues on food, about the safety of their farm workers and families, and about the spiraling use of increasingly ineffective chemicals, fifty California farmers founded California Certified Organic Farmers (CCOF) in 1973. Today, CCOF has about seven hundred farmer members whose agricultural practices meet the group's standards. What's more, the California Department of Food and Agriculture reports that about twenty-five hundred of the state's farms are registered organic, although not all of them have sought third-party certification.

In the context of California's enormous farm economy, organic production is minuscule—about 1 percent of total cash sales. But among California consumers, at least, demand appears to be strong. More grocery stores are offering at least a few organic items, and many farmers' markets offer a wide choice of organically grown fruits and vegetables. At the same time, a growing number of California chefs are seeking out organic produce, featuring it on their menus, and speaking out in support of the industry.

Organic farmers don't just avoid

The **Organic** Movement

chemicals. To meet CCOF standards, they also implement practices, such as planting cover crops, that restore the health of their soil and the biodiversity of their farms. Organic farmers are trying to build a balanced ecosystem, where beneficial insects eat the destructive ones, waste is recycled, and well-nourished plants can resist disease.

Grilled Teleme in Chard Leaves

4 large, unblemished Swiss chard
   leaves with no holes

boiling water as needed

6 oz (185 g) California teleme
   cheese, chilled and evenly divided
   into 4 slices

pinch of red pepper flakes

½ teaspoon chopped fresh oregano

4 slices coarse country bread, about
   ½ inch (12 mm) thick and 4 inches
   (10 cm) long

1 clove garlic, halved

2 tablespoons olive oil

salt to taste

I am a big fan of soft, creamy teleme cheese, especially when it is ripe and runny. As it is made in California, this cow's milk cheese has an edible, rice flour–dusted rind and an unctuous texture after a few weeks' aging. This is a knife-and-fork dish, to pair with a glass of Sauvignon Blanc.

1.   Prepare a medium-hot fire in a grill.

2.   Carefully cut away the white rib from each chard leaf, but leave each leaf in one piece. Put the leaves in a large bowl. Pour in boiling water to cover and let stand for 2 minutes. Transfer to a sieve to drain and place under cold running water until cold. Gently squeeze dry. Lay the chard leaves flat in a single layer on a kitchen towel and pat dry.

3.   Put one slice of cheese in the center of each leaf. Sprinkle each piece with a few red pepper flakes and then top evenly with the oregano. Fold the bottom end of each chard leaf over the cheese, fold in the sides, and roll up to form a neat package.

4.   Place the bread slices on the grill rack and grill, turning once, until toasted on both sides. Rub one side of each slice with a cut side of garlic. Drizzle the garlic-rubbed side of each slice with 1 teaspoon of the olive oil. Set aside on individual plates.

5.   Brush the cheese packages with the remaining 2 teaspoons olive oil and season with salt. Place on the grill rack directly over the coals and heat for 1 minute. Turn and grill on the second side until the cheese feels very soft to the touch, about 1 minute longer.

6.   Place a cheese package on each slice of bread and serve immediately.

SERVES 4

NUTRITIONAL ANALYSIS PER SERVING
Calories 269 (Kilojoules 1,130); Protein 11 g; Carbohydrates 17 g; Total Fat 18 g;
Saturated Fat 6 g; Cholesterol 15 mg; Sodium 496 mg; Dietary Fiber 2 g

Risotto with Fresh Corn and Basil Oil

2 or 3 ears of yellow corn, husks and silk removed

2 tablespoons unsalted butter

1 cup (3 oz/90 g) thinly sliced leeks, white and pale greens part only

2 cups (16 fl oz/500 ml) chicken stock

3 cups (24 fl oz/750 ml) water

1½ cups (10½ oz/330 g) Arborio rice

salt and freshly ground pepper to taste

2 tablespoons thinly sliced fresh chives

4 tablespoons (2 fl oz/60 ml) store-bought basil oil

Californians are so enamored of risotto that they have t[...] it in new directions, adding ingredients that would make most Italians shudder. But even Italians, who rarely eat sweet corn, would appreciate this variation. Offer it as a starter before a shrimp (prawn) or salmon main course or serve it in smaller portions as a side dish.

1. Holding each ear of corn by its pointed end, and steadying its stalk end on a cutting board, cut down along the ear with a sharp knife to strip off the kernels, turning the ear with each cut. You will need 1½ cups (9 oz/280 g) corn kernels. Set aside.

2. In a saucepan over medium heat, melt the butter. Add the leeks and stir to coat with the butter. Cover, reduce the heat to medium-low, and cook until wilted and soft, about 5 minutes. Check occasionally to make sure they are not burning.

3. Meanwhile, pour the stock and water into a saucepan and place over medium heat. Adjust the heat to keep the mixture hot but not simmering.

4. Raise the heat under the leeks to medium, add the rice, and cook, stirring constantly, until the rice is hot throughout, about 3 minutes. Begin adding the hot liquid ½ cup (4 fl oz/125 ml) at a time, stirring constantly and adding more liquid only when the previous addition has been absorbed. After 10 minutes, stir in the corn. It should take about 20 minutes for the rice to absorb all the liquid and become al dente. The risotto should be creamy, neither soupy nor stiff. If you need more liquid, use boiling water. Season with salt and pepper.

5. Remove from the heat and stir in the chives and 2 tablespoons of the basil oil. Divide the risotto among warmed bowls. Top with the remaining 2 tablespoons basil oil, dividing evenly. Serve immediately.

SERVES 4

NUTRITIONAL ANALYSIS PER SERVING
Calories 501 (Kilojoules 2,104); Protein 8 g; Carbohydrates 70 g; Total Fat 22 g; Saturated Fat 6 g; Cholesterol 16 mg; Sodium 515 mg; Dietary Fiber 7 g

Pizza with Smoked Salmon and Crème Fraîche

DOUGH

¼ cup (2 fl oz/60 ml) warm water (110°F/43°C)

1½ teaspoons active dry yeast

1 tablespoon olive oil

1 teaspoon salt

1½–2 cups (7½–10 oz/235–315 g) unbleached all-purpose (plain) flour

TOPPING

2 tablespoons unsalted butter

2 cups (6 oz/185 g) thinly sliced leeks, white and pale green parts only

salt and freshly ground pepper to taste

½ cup (4 fl oz/125 ml) crème fraîche, at room temperature

1½ tablespoons minced fresh dill

1 teaspoon prepared horseradish

yellow cornmeal for dusting

1½ tablespoons extra-virgin olive oil

6 oz (185 g) thinly sliced smoked salmon, at room temperature

4 lemon wedges

1. To make the dough, put the warm water in a large bowl. Sprinkle the yeast over the surface, let stand for 2 minutes, then stir until dissolved. Let stand until bubbly, about 10 minutes. Whisk in the olive oil and salt. Stir in 1½ cups (7½ oz/235 g) of the flour. Turn out the dough onto a lightly floured work surface and knead until smooth and elastic, about 5 minutes, using only as much of the remaining flour as needed to prevent sticking. Shape into a ball, transfer to an oiled bowl, turn the dough to coat it with oil, then cover tightly with plastic wrap and let rise at cool room temperature for about 2 hours. Punch down the dough, reshape into a ball, cover the bowl, and let the dough rise again for about 4 hours.

2. Position a rack in the center of the oven, then line it with baking tiles or a baking stone. Preheat to 550°F (290°C) for at least 45 minutes. Punch down the dough and turn it out onto a work surface. Shape into a ball. Cover with a clean kitchen towel and let rest for 30 minutes.

3. To make the topping, melt the butter in a frying pan over medium heat. Add the leeks, season with salt and pepper, and stir to coat. Cover, reduce the heat to medium-low, and cook until soft but not mushy, 7–8 minutes. Remove from the heat. In a small bowl, whisk together the crème fraîche, dill, and horseradish. Season with salt and pepper.

4. On a lightly floured work surface, roll out the dough into a 14-inch (35-cm) round. Transfer to a pizza peel or rimless baking sheet dusted with cornmeal. Spread the leeks evenly over the round, leaving a ¾-inch (2-cm) rim uncovered. Brush the rim with half of the olive oil.

5. Slide the pizza onto the baking tiles or stone. Bake until the crust is crisp and browned, 8–10 minutes. Transfer to a cutting board and brush the rim with the remaining olive oil. Dot the surface with the crème fraîche mixture, then spread it to cover the leeks. Arrange the smoked salmon on top. Cut into 8 wedges. Serve with lemon wedges on the side.

SERVES 4

NUTRITIONAL ANALYSIS PER SERVING
Calories 586 (Kilojoules 2,461); Protein 18 g; Carbohydrates 65 g; Total Fat 28 g; Saturated Fat 12 g; Cholesterol 50 mg; Sodium 1,466 mg; Dietary Fiber 3 g

Farmers'
Markets

In 1979, California had 21 state-certified farmers' markets. Only twenty years later, it had more than 350. No other statistic shows so clearly how much Californians care about fresh produce.

From one end of the state to the other, farmers' markets lure shoppers who seek value, variety, and freshness. In urban areas such as Los Angeles and the San Francisco Bay Area, it's possible to attend a different market every day of the week.

What has brought about the huge growth in this old-fashioned way of selling, a tradition that nearly vanished with the advent of suburbs and supermarkets? Farmers' market authorities say it is the quality. The figs are soft and ripe, the peaches smell like peaches, and the vine-ripened tomatoes remind older shoppers of tomatoes they haven't tasted since childhood.

Unlike growers who know their produce will be shipped long distances, those who farm for the farmers' market can pick their produce when it is ripe. Surveys indicate that farmers travel only fifty miles (80 km) on average to a market. Most vendors say they harvest their corn, pick their salad greens, or dig their beets the day before a market. For shoppers, this means maximum nutrition, maximum flavor, and maximum shelf life at home.

Many farmers' market patrons also appreciate the variety they find. In California, at the height of summer, a potato grower may bring six or eight unusual types, such as Bintjes, Yukon golds, Yellow Finns, or Ruby Crescents. At any one market, there may be fifteen different tomato varieties; a half-dozen different plums; Royal Anne and Rainier cherries, in addition to the commonplace Bings; and heirloom apple varieties not seen for half a century.

Over the last few years, many produce items have debuted at farmers' markets, such as green garlic, Tuscan kale (also called lacinato kale), Sun Gold cherry tomatoes, plumcots, and fingerling potatoes. Successful there, some have moved into conventional markets, broadening the produce experience for everyone.

Even within California, farmers' markets have distinctive characters, reflecting the local agriculture and community. In multicultural San Francisco, shoppers from every ethnic group roam the bustling Alemany Farmers Market, snapping up Indian fenugreek greens, Filipino jute greens, and Chinese jujubes. At the Santa Monica or Venice market in Southern California, swimsuit-clad customers shop on rollerblades. At Santa Barbara's beautiful market, growers bring avocados, grapefruits, cherimoyas, and other tropical fruits that thrive in that magical climate.

Farmers' markets offer the best of seasonal produce (opposite). Some vendors proffer bread, eggs, and homemade jam, honey, and oil (below).

Spicy Roasted Eggplant with Oyster Sauce

2 lb (1 kg) Asian (slender) eggplants (aubergines)

2 tablespoons oyster sauce

2 tablespoons Thai or Vietnamese fish sauce

1 tablespoon soy sauce

1 tablespoon sugar

3 tablespoons peanut oil

4 large cloves garlic, minced

1½ tablespoons peeled and finely minced fresh ginger

scant ½ teaspoon red pepper flakes

⅓ cup (½ oz/15 g) chopped fresh cilantro (fresh coriander)

2 teaspoons Asian sesame oil

California's Asian immigrants have introduced a vast repertoire of savory dishes made with the long, slender Chinese and Japanese eggplants. Here, ingredients from the Asian pantry—fish sauce, oyster sauce, pepper flakes, and sesame oil—turn mild-tasting roasted eggplant into an irresistible, tongue-tingling dish. Serve with pork or fish.

1. Preheat the oven to 475°F (245°C). Prick the eggplants in several places with a fork to allow steam to escape. Place on a baking sheet and bake until tender when pierced with a knife, about 25 minutes. Remove from the oven and slit the eggplant skins lengthwise with a knife to speed cooling. When cool, use a spoon to scrape the flesh from the skin in long, thick shreds. It's okay if some of the skin sticks to the flesh.

2. In a small bowl, whisk together the oyster sauce, fish sauce, soy sauce, and sugar, whisking until the sugar dissolves.

3. In a frying pan over medium heat, warm the peanut oil. Add the garlic, ginger, and red pepper flakes and cook, stirring, for about 1 minute to release the flavor of the aromatics. Add the shredded eggplant and cook, stirring, for 1 minute. Add the oyster sauce mixture and stir to combine. Cook for 1–2 minutes to blend the flavors.

4. Remove from the heat and stir in the cilantro and sesame oil. Let the eggplant cool in the pan.

5. Transfer to a serving dish and serve warm or at room temperature.

SERVES 4

NUTRITIONAL ANALYSIS PER SERVING
Calories 209 (Kilojoules 878); Protein 5 g; Carbohydrates 20 g; Total Fat 13 g; Saturated Fat 2 g; Cholesterol 0 mg; Sodium 921 mg; Dietary Fiber 3 g

Spaghetti with Sun-Dried Tomato Pesto

¼ cup (2 oz/60 g) whole unskinned almonds

¼ cup (1½ oz/45 g) oil-packed sun-dried tomatoes, drained

16 large fresh basil leaves

2 cloves garlic, minced

pinch of red pepper flakes

¼ cup (2 fl oz/60 ml) olive oil

½ cup (4 fl oz/125 ml) water

⅓ cup (1½ oz/45 g) plus 4 table-spoons (1 oz/30 g) grated pecorino cheese

salt to taste

1 lb (500 g) spaghetti

Italy may have invented sun-dried tomatoes, but California popularized them. In fact, these intensely sweet tomato nuggets have been so thoroughly embraced by California cooks that some critics say they are overused. In this nutty pesto, however, they are undeniably welcome.

1. Preheat the oven to 325°F (165°C).

2. Bring a small pot three-fourths full of water to a boil. Add the almonds and boil for 30 seconds. Drain, then immediately wrap the almonds in a kitchen towel and rub them in the towel to loosen the skins. Pinch the almonds from the skins; the almonds should slip out easily. Spread the almonds in a pie pan and toast, stirring once or twice, until golden brown and fragrant, about 30 minutes. Let cool.

3. In a food processor or blender, combine the almonds, tomatoes, basil, garlic, and red pepper flakes. Pulse until finely chopped. With the motor running, gradually add the olive oil, and then add the water. Blend until puréed but not completely smooth. Transfer to a large bowl and stir in the ⅓ cup (1½ oz/45 g) cheese and salt to taste.

4. Bring a large pot three-fourths full of salted water to a boil over high heat. Add the pasta, stir well, and cook until al dente, 10–12 minutes or according to package directions.

5. Just before the pasta is done, whisk about ⅔ cup (5 fl oz/160 ml) of the boiling pasta water into the pesto to thin it. Scoop out about ½ cup (4 fl oz/125 ml) of the boiling water and set aside.

6. Drain the pasta and transfer it to the bowl holding the sauce. Toss well, adding a little of the hot water if needed to thin the sauce. Divide the pasta among warmed bowls. Top each portion with 1 tablespoon of the remaining cheese. Serve immediately.

SERVES 4

NUTRITIONAL ANALYSIS PER SERVING
Calories 728 (Kilojoules 3,058); Protein 25 g; Carbohydrates 92 g; Total Fat 30 g; Saturated Fat 6 g; Cholesterol 18 mg; Sodium 668 mg; Dietary Fiber 5 g

White Bean Purée with Rosemary

2 cups (12 oz/375 g) dried Gigandes
or other large dried white beans

6 cups (48 fl oz/1.5 l) water

½ yellow onion

1 celery stalk, cut into thirds

1 bay leaf

salt and freshly ground pepper to taste

⅓ cup (3 fl oz/80 ml) extra-virgin
olive oil

3 cloves garlic, minced

1 teaspoon minced fresh rosemary

In recent years, lowly beans have come to the fore in California kitchens, especially if the beans are heirlooms. These old-fashioned varieties, which a few small growers have revived, are revered for their taste, their texture, or their striking coloring. Serve this purée with grilled lamb or sausages.

1. Pick over the beans to remove any stones and rinse well. Place in a bowl with water to cover by about 2 inches (5 cm) and let soak overnight.

2. The next day, drain the beans and put them in a pot with the water, onion, celery, and bay leaf. Bring to a simmer over medium-high heat, cover, and adjust the heat to maintain a bare simmer. Cook until the beans are tender, about 1 hour. Remove from the heat, season with salt and pepper, and let cool in the liquid.

3. In a large frying pan over medium heat, warm the olive oil. Add the garlic and rosemary and sauté until the garlic is fragrant and lightly colored, about 1 minute. Using a slotted spoon, lift the beans out of the liquid and add them to the frying pan. Reserve the liquid. Season the beans with salt and pepper and stir to coat with the seasonings. Simmer gently for 5 minutes to blend the flavors.

4. Working in batches, transfer the contents of the frying pan to a food processor and purée until smooth. Add the reserved bean-cooking liquid as necessary to make a purée of appealing consistency. Taste and adjust the seasonings if necessary.

5. Serve immediately. You can also make the purée up to 2 hours in advance and reheat it in a saucepan, adding additional bean-cooking liquid as needed to thin.

SERVES 4

NUTRITIONAL ANALYSIS PER SERVING
Calories 456 (Kilojoules 1,915); Protein 20 g; Carbohydrates 54 g; Total Fat 19 g;
Saturated Fat 3 g; Cholesterol 0 mg; Sodium 23 mg; Dietary Fiber 9 g

Artichokes are practically a California mascot. The state grows virtually all of the country's domestic crop, and it's thought that Californians consume almost half of it. March through May, when the harvest peaks, many markets showcase huge mounds of the shapely artichokes, and few shoppers leave without some.

Although the Spanish introduced the vegetable, commercial production didn't really get underway until southern European immigrants established some plantings in Half Moon Bay, south of San Francisco, in the 1880s. Later, the main production area moved farther south, to the area around Castroville, which now bills itself as the Artichoke Capital of the World.

Today, the state's growers cultivate about nine thousand acres (3,600 hectares) of this prickly silvery-gray thistle, mostly in a foggy belt along the central coast. Each plant produces artichokes—flower buds, actually—in a range of sizes, from hefty jumbos to two-ounce (60 g) "babies." In fact, baby artichokes are fully mature; they just grow lower on the plant where they get less sun. They have no prickly choke, so

Artichokes

after trimming, you can eat the whole thing.

On most farms, commercial artichokes are a perennial plant, propagated by cuttings. In recent years, however, researchers have developed seed varieties that could dramatically change the industry. Grown as annuals, these new discoveries could be planted and harvested year-round.

Potato-Rosemary Focaccia

SPONGE

1 cup (8 fl oz/250 ml) warm water (110°F/43°C)

1 teaspoon active dry yeast

1 cup (5 oz/155 g) unbleached all-purpose (plain) flour

FOCACCIA

the sponge

½ cup (4 fl oz/125 ml) water

⅓ cup (3 fl oz/80 ml) dry white wine

⅓ cup (3 fl oz/80 ml) olive oil

2 tablespoons yellow cornmeal

1½ teaspoons kosher salt

2¾ cups (14 oz/440 g) unbleached all-purpose (plain) flour

2 teaspoons plus 3 tablespoons extra-virgin olive oil

½ lb (250 g) Yukon gold or other small waxy potatoes

1 large clove garlic, minced

kosher salt and freshly ground pepper to taste

1½ teaspoons minced fresh rosemary

1. To make the sponge, put the warm water in a bowl, sprinkle the yeast over it and let stand for 2 minutes, then stir until dissolved. Stir in the flour until smooth. Cover and let stand at room temperature for 24 hours.

2. To make the dough, put the sponge in the bowl of a stand mixer fitted with a paddle attachment. Add the water, wine, olive oil, cornmeal, and salt and mix on low speed until blended. Gradually mix in the flour to make a soft dough. Increase the speed to medium and knead for about 5 minutes. Cover the bowl with plastic wrap and let the dough rise at room temperature until doubled, about 1½ hours.

3. Generously grease a 12-by-17-inch (30-by-43-cm) rimmed baking sheet with the 2 teaspoons olive oil. Transfer the dough to the baking sheet and, with oiled fingers, pat and stretch it to cover the sheet. It will be too elastic to cover it completely, and will bounce back. Let the dough rest for 5 minutes, then stretch again. If it still refuses to cover, let rest again for 5–10 minutes, then stretch once more. Let rise, uncovered, until puffy, about 1½ hours.

4. Position a rack in the center of the oven, then line it with baking tiles or a baking stone. Preheat to 550°F (290°C) for at least 45 minutes.

5. In a saucepan, combine the potatoes with salted water to cover, bring to a boil, and cook until just tender when pierced, about 20 minutes. Drain and let cool, then slice ¼ inch (6 mm) thick. In a bowl, toss the potato slices with 1 tablespoon of the olive oil, the garlic, salt, and pepper.

6. Using a brush, gently daub the dough with the remaining 2 tablespoons olive oil. Top evenly with the potato slices, pressing them gently into the dough. Sprinkle the surface with the rosemary and kosher salt.

7. Bake until browned and firm, 15–20 minutes. Slide the focaccia onto a wire rack. Serve warm or at room temperature, cut into squares.

SERVES 8

NUTRITIONAL ANALYSIS PER SERVING
Calories 412 (Kilojoules 1,730); Protein 8 g; Carbohydrates 59 g; Total Fat 16 g; Saturated Fat 2 g; Cholesterol 0 mg; Sodium 280 mg; Dietary Fiber 3 g

Steakhouse Creamed Spinach

2 lb (1 kg) spinach, thick stems removed

1½ tablespoons unsalted butter

1½ tablespoons all-purpose (plain) flour

¾ cup (6 fl oz/180 ml) milk

¼ cup (2 fl oz/60 ml) heavy (double) cream

1 clove garlic, halved and lightly crushed

salt and freshly ground pepper to taste

2 teaspoons Pernod, or more to taste

California, so well known for inventive cuisine, has some treasured old-fashioned steakhouses, too. At establishments such as the House of Prime Rib, Alfred's, Harris', or Lawry's, diners feast on prime rib or thick, dry-aged porterhouse steaks and, quite likely, a side dish of creamed spinach. Pernod, an anise-flavored aperitif, adds an appealing accent to the spinach.

1. Place the spinach in a large pot with just the rinsing water clinging to the leaves. Cover and cook over medium heat until the spinach just wilts, about 4 minutes. Drain in a sieve, then flush with cold running water to cool quickly. Drain well, pressing against the spinach with the back of a spoon, then squeeze dry. Chop finely and set aside.

2. In a saucepan over medium heat, melt the butter. Sprinkle in the flour, whisk to blend, and cook for 1 minute, whisking constantly. Add the milk, cream, and garlic and bring to a simmer, whisking until smooth. Reduce the heat to low and cook, whisking often, for 5 minutes to eliminate any floury taste.

3. Stir in the spinach with a wooden spoon and season with salt and pepper. Cook, stirring often, for 10 minutes to blend the flavors.

4. Remove the garlic halves and discard. Stir in the 2 teaspoons Pernod, taste, and adjust with salt, pepper, and Pernod.

5. Transfer to a warmed bowl and serve immediately.

SERVES 4

NUTRITIONAL ANALYSIS PER SERVING
Calories 171 (Kilojoules 718); Protein 7 g; Carbohydrates 11 g; Total Fat 12 g; Saturated Fat 7 g; Cholesterol 38 mg; Sodium 158 mg; Dietary Fiber 4 g

Fettuccine with Mushrooms and Truffle Oil

1½ lb (750 g) fresh wild mushrooms of one kind, such as chanterelles, oyster mushrooms, or morels, brushed clean and thinly sliced

6 tablespoons (3 oz/90 g) unsalted butter

salt and freshly ground pepper to taste

about ¾ cup (6 fl oz/180 ml) veal stock or best-quality canned beef broth, if needed to moisten the mushrooms, plus 1½ cups (12 fl oz/375 ml)

4 cloves garlic, minced

¼ cup (⅓ oz/10 g) minced fresh flat-leaf (Italian) parsley

1 lb (500 g) fresh fettuccine

1 tablespoon black or white truffle oil

California chefs have fallen for truffle oil, sprinkling this earthy, concentrated essence on everything from carpaccio to mashed potatoes. The oil is expensive, but it doesn't take much to impart a powerful truffle fragrance.

1. Preheat the oven to the lowest setting. Put a large bowl in the oven to warm. Bring a large pot three-fourths full of salted water to a boil.

2. Heat a 12-inch (30-cm) frying pan over high heat until very hot and add the mushrooms. They will soon begin to release moisture and will not stick. Cut 4 tablespoons (2 oz/60 g) of the butter into small pieces and add to the pan. Season the mushrooms highly with salt and pepper. Sauté over high or medium-high heat until all the mushroom juices have evaporated and the mushrooms begin to sizzle and brown, about 15 minutes. Reduce the heat if the mushrooms threaten to burn. If they do not release much moisture and cook dry before they are tender, add a little of the stock or broth. Continue cooking until tender, adding more stock or broth, a little at a time, if necessary. Add the garlic and sauté for 2 minutes to release its fragrance. Stir in the parsley. Transfer the mushrooms to the warmed bowl and return the bowl to the warm oven.

3. Add the 1½ cups (12 fl oz/375 ml) stock or broth to the frying pan and deglaze over medium-high heat, scraping up any browned bits on the pan bottom with a wooden spoon. Simmer until the stock is reduced by half. Adjust the heat so the stock stays warm without reducing further.

4. Add the pasta to the boiling water, stir well, and cook until al dente, 1–2 minutes. Drain and immediately transfer to the pan with the stock. Add the remaining 2 tablespoons butter and the truffle oil and toss well.

5. Add the fettuccine to the mushrooms and toss again. Serve immediately on warmed individual plates.

SERVES 4

NUTRITIONAL ANALYSIS PER SERVING
Calories 566 (Kilojoules 2,377); Protein 18 g; Carbohydrates 72 g; Total Fat 24 g; Saturated Fat 12 g; Cholesterol 131 mg; Sodium 882 mg; Dietary Fiber 5 g

Orecchiette with Fava Beans

4 lb (2 kg) fava (broad) beans, shelled

⅓ cup (3 fl oz/80 ml) extra-virgin olive oil

1 cup (6 oz/185 g) minced red (Spanish) onion

2 cups (12 oz/375 g) neatly diced peeled tomato

2 tablespoons chopped fresh flat-leaf (Italian) parsley

pinch of red pepper flakes

salt and freshly ground black pepper to taste

1 lb (500 g) dried orecchiette (ear-shaped pasta)

½ cup (2 oz/60 g) grated pecorino cheese

Years ago, I could find fava beans only in the small groceries of North Beach, San Francisco's Italian neighborhood. Now, with the wave of interest in Mediterranean cooking, these flavorful beans are on many chefs' shopping lists and in the bins of farmers' markets throughout the state.

1. Bring a saucepan three-fourths full of water to a boil over high heat. Drop in the fava beans and boil for 30 seconds if small, or for up to 1 minute if large. Drain and immerse in ice water to stop the cooking. When cool, drain again. Pinch open the end of each bean opposite the end that connected it to the pod. The beans will slip easily from their skins.

2. Bring a large pot three-fourths full of salted water to a boil over high heat.

3. Meanwhile, in a large frying pan over medium heat, warm the olive oil. Add the onion and sauté until softened, about 5 minutes. Add the tomato, parsley, and red pepper flakes and season generously with salt and black pepper. Cook, stirring occasionally, until the tomato just softens, about 3 minutes. Do not allow the tomato to collapse and form a sauce. Add the fava beans and stir to coat with the seasonings; adjust the heat to keep the sauce warm.

4. Add the pasta to the boiling water, stir well, and cook until al dente, about 11 minutes or according to package directions. Drain and return to the warm pot. Add the tomato mixture and toss well. Add the cheese and toss again.

5. Divide among warmed individual bowls and serve immediately.

SERVES 4–6

NUTRITIONAL ANALYSIS PER SERVING
Calories 626 (Kilojoules 2,629); Protein 24 g; Carbohydrates 89 g; Total Fat 21 g; Saturated Fat 5 g; Cholesterol 11 mg; Sodium 525 mg; Dietary Fiber 9 g

Years ago, if you wanted favas, you had to grow them yourself or seek them out in markets that catered to an Italian clientele. In San Francisco's North Beach neighborhood, they would show up occasionally in spring and fall, but you had to beat the Italian housewives to them.

The beans do well in the cool, coastal farmland around Pescadero and Half Moon Bay, where many Italian and Portuguese immigrants settled. Favas are a staple in their cooking, and for decades most of the favas grown there stayed within that community. But in recent years, as California's fascination with Mediterranean cooking has grown, more growers are bringing fava beans to market. Southern California shoppers can find them at the lively Santa Monica farmers' market, brought in from Oxnard and Oceanside. Los Angeles chefs feature them prominently in their Mediterranean-inspired dishes.

In hot-summer areas, the beans are planted in winter for spring harvest. In cool-summer areas like Pescadero, they are planted in spring for the fall. The beans need to be removed from their thick, fuzzy pods

Fava **Beans**

before cooking. When they are young and tender, you can simply shell them and eat them raw with pecorino cheese or cook them briefly without peeling. Older beans should be double peeled, that is, removed from the pods, then blanched and slipped out of their skins. The bright green fava inside is one of nature's prettiest sights.

Portobello Mushrooms with Soft Polenta

POLENTA

7½ cups (60 fl oz/1.9 l) water

salt to taste

1½ cups (7½ oz/235 g) polenta

freshly ground pepper to taste

1½ tablespoons unsalted butter

MUSHROOMS

¼ cup (2 fl oz/60 ml) olive oil

4 large cloves garlic, minced

2 teaspoons minced fresh thyme

2 tablespoons balsamic vinegar

salt and freshly ground pepper to taste

4 fresh portobello mushrooms, each about 5 oz (155 g) and 5 inches (13 cm) in diameter

¼ cup (2 oz/60 g) unsalted butter, at room temperature

2 tablespoons minced fresh flat-leaf (Italian) parsley

Health-conscious California diners trying to cut back on meat have embraced outsized portobello mushrooms. Cooked and sliced like a steak and served over polenta with garlic butter, they make a satisfying—if not particularly low-calorie—meatless meal.

1. To make the polenta, in a saucepan, combine the water and salt and bring to a boil over high heat. Whisking constantly, add the polenta in a slow, steady stream. When the mixture thickens, reduce the heat so the polenta bubbles gently. Cook, stirring often with a wooden spoon, until the polenta is smooth and no longer gritty, about 45 minutes. Season with salt and pepper and stir in the butter.

2. Meanwhile, prepare the mushrooms: Preheat the broiler (griller) and position a rack 8 inches (20 cm) from the heat source. In a small frying pan over medium heat, warm the olive oil. Add all but 2 teaspoons of the garlic and sauté for 1 minute. Remove from the heat, add the thyme, and let cool slightly. Whisk in the vinegar, salt, and pepper.

3. Lightly oil a baking sheet and place the mushrooms, gill sides up, on it. Brush with about half of the oil-vinegar mixture. Broil (grill) until sizzling, about 5 minutes. Turn the mushrooms over and brush with the remaining oil-vinegar mixture. Set the oven temperature to 425°F (220°C). Bake until tender when pierced, about 15 minutes.

4. While the mushrooms bake, combine the butter, the reserved 2 teaspoons garlic, the parsley, salt, and pepper. Mix until smooth.

5. Divide the polenta among warmed plates or shallow bowls. Slice the mushrooms at a 45-degree angle, as you would slice a flank steak, and place the mushrooms and any juices atop the polenta. Top each mushroom with one-fourth of the seasoned butter. Let stand briefly to melt the butter, then spread it over the mushrooms. Serve immediately.

SERVES 4

NUTRITIONAL ANALYSIS PER SERVING
Calories 497 (Kilojoules 2,087); Protein 8 g; Carbohydrates 50 g; Total Fat 31 g; Saturated Fat 12 g; Cholesterol 43 mg; Sodium 11 mg; Dietary Fiber 5 g

4 Desserts

In a state that produces fresh fruit year-round, it's natural that fruit desserts reign. In summer, a cook might turn fragrant berries into an improvisational crisp (page 122) or showcase plums and peaches in a French-style galette (page 130). The arrival of fall means the last of the figs, exquisite when baked (page 128), and the first of the pomegranates. In winter, citrus fruits offer the possibility of a refreshing fruit salad finale (page 134), and spring promises a flood of strawberries for rich, crumbly shortcakes (page 136). But despite this parade of fruits, Californians are incurable chocoholics. Indeed, most restaurateurs say they wouldn't dream of writing a menu without a chocolate dessert.

Mixed Berry Crisp

TOPPING

½ cup (2 oz/60 g) walnut pieces

¾ cup (4 oz/125 g) unbleached all-purpose (plain) flour

3 tablespoons firmly packed brown sugar

2 tablespoons granulated sugar

¼ teaspoon ground cinnamon

pinch of salt

6 tablespoons (3 oz/90 g) unsalted butter, cut into small pieces

⅓ cup (1 oz/30 g) old-fashioned rolled oats

FILLING

6 cups (1½ lb/750 g) mixed berries such as raspberries, blackberries, loganberries, and olallieberries, in any combination

¾ cup (6 oz/185 g) granulated sugar, or to taste

¼ cup (1 oz/30 g) quick-cooking tapioca

A California summer announces itself in a flood of berries. I like to bring home a berry medley and make a mixed-fruit crisp to serve with vanilla ice cream.

1. To make the topping, preheat the oven to 325°F (165°C). Spread the walnuts on a baking sheet and toast until fragrant and lightly colored, about 25 minutes. Let cool and then chop coarsely. Raise the oven temperature to 375°F (190°C).

2. In an electric mixer fitted with the paddle attachment, combine the flour, brown and granulated sugars, cinnamon, and salt. Mix on low speed until blended. Add the butter and mix until the flour-coated pieces of butter are the size of peas. Add the walnuts and oats and mix on medium-low speed until the mixture begins to clump; it may take 2–3 minutes. Cover and refrigerate until needed.

3. To make the filling, in a large bowl, combine the berries, ¾ cup (6 oz/185 g) granulated sugar, and tapioca. Stir gently with a large rubber spatula, then let stand for 15 minutes. Taste and add more sugar, if desired.

4. Pour the filling into a 10-inch (25-cm) pie plate or an oval baking dish about 13 inches (33 cm) long by 8 inches (20 cm) wide. Top evenly with the walnut mixture.

5. Bake until the filling is bubbling and the topping is lightly browned, 55–60 minutes. Let cool for 30 minutes before serving.

SERVES 6

NUTRITIONAL ANALYSIS PER SERVING
Calories 476 (Kilojoules 1,999); Protein 5 g; Carbohydrates 77 g; Total Fat 18 g; Saturated Fat 8 g; Cholesterol 31 mg; Sodium 52 mg; Dietary Fiber 7 g

Chocolate, Orange, and Almond Cake

1 cup (5½ oz/170 g) plus 2 tablespoons whole blanched almonds

¾ cup (6 oz/185 g) sugar

6 eggs, separated

1 teaspoon vanilla extract (essence)

1 teaspoon grated orange zest

¾ cup (6 oz/185 g) unsalted butter

6 oz (185 g) bittersweet chocolate,
coarsely chopped

Apart from the flour used on the pan, this is a flourless cake with the moist, dense character that chocolate lovers crave. Ground almonds give it structure; orange zest enlivens the taste.

1. Preheat the oven to 375°F (190°C). Butter the bottom and sides of a 9-inch (23-cm) springform pan. Coat the bottom and sides with flour and tap out the excess.

2. In a food processor, combine the almonds with 1 tablespoon of the sugar and process until finely ground. Take care not to grind to a paste. Set aside.

3. Measure out 2 tablespoons of the sugar and set aside. In a bowl, using an electric mixer, beat together the egg yolks, the remaining sugar, the vanilla, and orange zest until pale and thick, 4–5 minutes.

4. In a small saucepan over low heat, melt the butter. Remove from the heat and add the chocolate. Let stand until the chocolate softens, 2–3 minutes, then stir until smooth.

5. In a large bowl, whisk the egg whites until soft peaks form. Gradually add the reserved 2 tablespoons sugar, whisking continuously until the whites are firm and glossy.

6. Add the chocolate mixture to the egg yolk mixture, then beat on medium-low speed until well blended, stopping to scrape down the sides of the bowl once or twice. Add the almonds and beat just until blended. Transfer the mixture to a large bowl. Using a rubber spatula, gently fold in the egg whites until just combined. Pour into the prepared pan.

7. Bake until the center is firm to the touch and the surface begins to crack, about 50 minutes. Transfer to a rack and let cool completely in the pan. To serve, remove the pan sides and slide the cake onto a serving plate.

SERVES 12

NUTRITIONAL ANALYSIS PER SERVING
Calories 356 (Kilojoules 1,495); Protein 7 g; Carbohydrates 26 g; Total Fat 27 g; Saturated Fat 12 g; Cholesterol 139 mg; Sodium 35 mg; Dietary Fiber 2 g

Dried-Fruit Compote with Mascarpone

2 cups (16 fl oz/500 ml) dry white wine

1 cup (8 oz/250 g) sugar

1 cup (8 fl oz/250 ml) water

1-inch (2.5-cm) piece vanilla bean, halved lengthwise

1 whole clove

2 lemon zest strips

1 lb (500 g) dried fruits *(see note)*

1½ tablespoons brandy, or to taste

½ cup (4 oz/125 g) mascarpone cheese

For the prettiest results, use a mixture of dried fruits, aiming for a contrast of sizes and colors. Farmers' markets often have the best-quality fruit, dried by the growers themselves. Look for nectarines, peaches, apricots, pears, prunes, figs, cherries, and golden raisins (sultanas). Note that you will need to cook the fruits separately by type as they require different cooking times.

1. In a saucepan, combine the wine, sugar, and water. Using a knife tip, scrape the seeds from the piece of vanilla bean into the saucepan, then add the pod as well. Add the clove and lemon zest strips. Bring the mixture to a simmer over medium heat, stirring to dissolve the sugar.

2. One variety at a time, gently poach the dried fruits in the syrup, covering the saucepan, until the fruit is plump and tender but not mushy. As each fruit is done, transfer it with a slotted spoon to a bowl. The timing will depend on the size and dryness of the fruit, but nectarines and figs may take 20–30 minutes, while raisins will take only 5 minutes. Quarter the larger poached fruits such as figs, pears, and nectarines; halve the smaller fruits such as apricots.

3. When all the fruits are poached, remove the syrup from the heat and let cool completely. Stir in the brandy. Strain over the fruits. Cover and refrigerate to chill thoroughly.

4. At serving time, in a small bowl, whisk the mascarpone, adding enough of the poaching syrup—2–3 tablespoons—to give it the consistency of softly whipped cream.

5. Divide the fruits and remaining syrup among balloon wineglasses. Top each serving with a dollop of mascarpone.

SERVES 6

NUTRITIONAL ANALYSIS PER SERVING
Calories 432 (Kilojoules 1,814); Protein 3 g; Carbohydrates 90 g; Total Fat 9 g; Saturated Fat 6 g; Cholesterol 16 mg; Sodium 19 mg; Dietary Fiber 5 g

Baked Figs with Honey Ice Cream

ICE CREAM

1½ cups (12 fl oz/375 ml) half-and-half (half cream)

1½ cups (12 fl oz/375 ml) heavy (double) cream

6 egg yolks

½ cup (6 oz/185 g) plus 2 tablespoons honey

1 tablespoon unsalted butter, cut into small pieces

12 large or 18 small ripe figs, halved lengthwise

1 tablespoon sugar

Many fig varieties produce two crops a year, one in early summer and another in late summer or early fall. California's farmers' markets are the best place to sample the harvests, as ripe figs are so fragile that they suffer when shipped far from the farm. Enjoy them out of hand, sliced and served with yogurt and honey, or baked, as described here.

1. To make the ice cream, in a saucepan over medium heat, combine the half-and-half and the heavy cream and heat until almost boiling. While the cream heats, in a large bowl, whisk together the egg yolks and honey until smooth. Gradually whisk in half of the hot cream, then return the mixture to the saucepan and cook over medium heat, stirring constantly, until the mixture visibly thickens and forms a custard, about 3 minutes. Do not let it boil, or it will curdle. Remove from the heat, let cool, and then refrigerate to chill thoroughly.

2. Freeze the custard in an ice-cream maker according to the manufacturer's directions. Store in the freezer until needed.

3. To bake the figs, preheat the oven to 425°F (220°C). Choose a baking dish large enough to hold the halved figs in a single layer. Dot the bottom of the dish with the butter.

4. Arrange the figs in the prepared dish, cut sides up, and sprinkle with the sugar. Bake until bubbling hot and tender, about 15 minutes.

5. Divide half of the figs among dessert goblets, balloon wineglasses, or compote dishes. Top each serving with some of the ice cream, the remaining figs, and any syrupy juices in the baking dish. You will have ice cream left over. Serve immediately.

SERVES 6

NUTRITIONAL ANALYSIS PER SERVING
Calories 570 (Kilojoules 2,394); Protein 7 g; Carbohydrates 60 g; Total Fat 36 g; Saturated Fat 21 g; Cholesterol 322 mg; Sodium 57 mg; Dietary Fiber 4 g

With the overwhelming majority of the crop destined for drying, fresh figs are a high-priced pleasure, even in California. But given that the state grows virtually the country's entire commercial crop and that ripe figs don't ship well, California is the place to try them.

In fact, the state's history is intertwined with the fig. Spanish missionaries introduced the tree, first planting it at Mission San Diego in the late 1700s. Moving north, they planted the handsome trees at each new outpost they established.

Today, California growers still cultivate what are now known as Mission figs, with their purple-black skins and sweet red flesh. The other commonly grown fig is the Calimyrna, a golden fig identical to the Turkish Smyrna but renamed by California growers after its introduction in the late 1800s. Patrons of farmers' markets may also find Kadotas, plump figs with yellowish green skin and amber flesh.

Mission fig trees produce two crops a year, an early harvest in June and another crop in late summer. Workers clamber up ladders to pick the fruits, wearing gloves to protect

Fresh **Figs**

their hands from the irritating milky sap that oozes from the stem.

Ideally, figs should ripen on the tree because they don't ripen after harvest. You will find them at their best at farmers' markets, or at produce markets or restaurants that buy from local growers. Enjoy them with prosciutto as an appetizer or with sugar and cream for dessert.

Peach and Plum Galette

PASTRY DOUGH

2 cups (10 oz/315 g) unbleached all-
 purpose (plain) flour

¾ teaspoon salt

½ cup (4 oz/125 g) chilled unsalted
 butter, cut into small pieces

7 tablespoons (3½ oz/105 g) chilled
 solid vegetable shortening, cut into
 small pieces

about ¼ cup (2 fl oz/60 ml) ice
 water

1 lb (500 g) peaches, halved, pitted,
 and cut into slices ⅓ inch (9 mm)
 thick

½ lb (250 g) plums, halved, pitted,
 and cut into slices ⅓ inch (9 mm)
 thick

2 tablespoons granulated sugar

1 egg yolk whisked with 1 teaspoon
 water

about 1 tablespoon coarse sugar

To make this rustic French tart, look for ripe, locally grown peaches and plums. Some of my favorites are the yellow O'Henry peach and the red-fleshed Elephant Heart plum.

1. To make the dough, in a food processor, combine the flour and salt and pulse two or three times to mix. Add the butter and pulse a few times until the flour-coated butter pieces are about the size of large peas. Add the shortening and pulse a few more times just until all the fat pieces are coated with flour. Transfer to a large bowl. Sprinkle the ice water over the mixture while tossing with a fork until the dough begins to come together. If necessary, knead the dough briefly in the bowl just until it coheres. Shape into a flat disk and cover tightly with plastic wrap. Refrigerate for at least 2 hours or as long as 24 hours.

2. Preheat the oven to 425°F (220°C). Turn out the dough on a lightly floured work surface. Cover with a fresh sheet of plastic wrap and let rest for 10–15 minutes. With the plastic wrap on top, roll out the dough into a rough 15-inch (38-cm) round.

3. Transfer the round to a rimless baking sheet, and trim the edges to make a neat 15-inch (38-cm) round. Working 2 inches (5 cm) in from the rim, make a circle of overlapping peach slices. Fill the center of the round with overlapping plum slices, arranging them neatly and tightly. You may not need all the slices. Sprinkle the fruit with the 2 tablespoons granulated sugar. Fold the edge of the dough up over the fruit to make a broad rim. Brush the rim with the egg-water mixture, then sprinkle with the coarse sugar.

4. Bake until the crust is golden brown and the fruit is tender, about 50 minutes. Slide a long knife under the galette to dislodge it if necessary, then transfer to a rack to cool briefly before serving.

SERVES 8

NUTRITIONAL ANALYSIS PER SERVING
Calories 403 (Kilojoules 1,693); Protein 5 g; Carbohydrates 41 g; Total Fat 25 g;
Saturated Fat 11 g; Cholesterol 58 mg; Sodium 221 mg; Dietary Fiber 2 g

Walnut-Raisin Biscotti

½ cup (3 oz/90 g) raisins

½ cup (4 fl oz/125 ml) warm water

1½ cups (6 oz/185 g) walnut pieces

2 cups (10 oz/315 g) all-purpose
(plain) flour

1 tablespoon aniseeds

1½ teaspoons baking powder

¼ teaspoon salt

½ cup (4 oz/125 g) unsalted butter,
at room temperature

1 cup (8 oz/250 g) sugar

2 eggs

1 tablespoon brandy

2 teaspoons vanilla extract (essence)

Until Bonnie Tempesta, a young San Franciscan, began making biscotti commercially in 1983, few non–Italian Americans had ever heard of these twice-baked cookies. Now biscotti fill cookie jars in bakeries and cafés across the country.

1. In a bowl, combine the raisins and warm water and let stand until soft, about 1 hour. Drain and set aside.

2. Preheat the oven to 325°F (165°C). Spread the walnuts on a baking sheet and toast until fragrant and lightly colored, about 25 minutes. Let cool, then chop coarsely. Leave the oven on. Line a large, heavy baking sheet with parchment (baking) paper.

3. In a bowl, stir together the flour, aniseeds, baking powder, and salt. In a large bowl, using an electric mixer set on medium speed, beat together the butter and sugar until light and fluffy, about 3 minutes. Add the eggs one at a time, beating well after each addition. Beat in the brandy and vanilla. Reduce the speed to low and add the flour mixture gradually, beating just until blended. Beat in the walnuts and drained raisins.

4. Using two large spoons, transfer the dough to the prepared baking sheet. Divide it into 3 equal portions. Using the backs of the spoons or floured fingertips, shape each portion into a log about 14 inches (35 cm) long and 1½ inches (4 cm) in diameter. The dough will be sticky.

5. Bake until firm to the touch and lightly colored, about 40 minutes. Remove from the oven and let stand for 15 minutes, then transfer to a cutting board. Using a serrated knife, cut on the diagonal into slices ⅜ inch (1 cm) wide. Transfer to an unlined baking sheet, cut side down, and bake, in batches, until lightly colored and dry, 15–20 minutes. Transfer to a rack to cool. As they cool, they will become crisp. Store in a covered container.

MAKES ABOUT 7 DOZEN COOKIES

NUTRITIONAL ANALYSIS PER COOKIE
Calories 51 (Kilojoules 214); Protein 1 g; Carbohydrates 7 g; Total Fat 2 g;
Saturated Fat 1 g; Cholesterol 8 mg; Sodium 18 mg; Dietary Fiber 0 g

Winter Fruits in Ginger Syrup

2 large navel oranges

1 ruby grapefruit

1 cup (8 fl oz/250 ml) water

1 cup (8 fl oz/250 ml) white wine

1 cup (8 oz/250 g) sugar

3 slices fresh ginger, peeled and smashed

1 whole clove

2 ripe but firm pears

½ cup (2 oz/60 g) pomegranate seeds

California's winter fruits—citrus, pomegranates, and pears—marry well in a light ginger syrup. How do you recognize a sweet pomegranate? Look for those with cracks, which indicate that the fruit is almost bursting with juice.

1. Using a vegetable peeler, remove 4 strips of orange zest and set aside. Cut a slice off the top and bottom of 1 orange to expose the flesh. Stand the orange upright on a cutting board and, using a sharp knife, thickly slice off the peel, cutting around the contour of the fruit to expose the flesh. Holding the orange over a large bowl, cut along both sides of each orange section to free it, allowing the sections to drop into the bowl. Holding the remaining orange membrane over a saucepan, squeeze it to extract any juice. Repeat with the second orange and the grapefruit, putting the sections in the same bowl and any juice in the saucepan. When you have finished preparing the citrus fruits, pour any collected juices in the bowl into the saucepan.

2. Add the 4 strips of orange zest to the saucepan along with the water, wine, sugar, ginger, and clove. Place over medium heat and bring to a simmer, stirring to dissolve the sugar. Cook, uncovered, until reduced to 2 cups (16 fl oz/500 ml), about 15 minutes.

3. Peel, quarter, and core the pears. Cut each quarter lengthwise into 2 or 3 slices. Add the pears to the saucepan, cover, and cook at a gentle simmer until barely tender, about 1 minute. They will continue to cook as they cool. Using a slotted spoon, transfer the pears to the bowl holding the citrus fruits. Add the pomegranate seeds.

4. Let the syrup cool completely, then strain over the fruit. Cover and refrigerate to chill thoroughly before serving.

5. Spoon into small glass bowls to serve.

SERVES 4

NUTRITIONAL ANALYSIS PER SERVING
Calories 380 (Kilojoules 1,596); Protein 2 g; Carbohydrates 88 g; Total Fat 1 g; Saturated Fat 0 g; Cholesterol 0 mg; Sodium 5 mg; Dietary Fiber 5 g

California's Central Valley boasts some of the world's richest farmland. Nearly seven million acres (2,800,000 hectares) of irrigated cropland stretch from Redding to Bakersfield, yielding an impressive share of the nation's food and fiber. Of the country's top eleven agricultural counties, six are in the Central Valley.

Thanks to fertile soil, favorable weather, and available (if not abundant) water, the valley supports a remarkably diverse agriculture, with farmers growing grapes, lettuce, tomatoes, oranges, asparagus, rice, wheat, peaches, prunes, walnuts, almonds, and pistachios. It's also dairy and cattle country.

In the last fifty years, irrigation has transformed this landscape. Before then, the valley supported primarily grains and livestock. But state and federal water projects have made a much larger range of crops possible, carefully allocating what will always be a scarce local resource.

By most definitions, the Central Valley includes both the Sacramento Valley in the north and the San Joaquin Valley in the south. Rice, prunes, and tree nuts thrive in the north, while the south produces the

Central **Valley**

lion's share of the nation's table, raisin, and wine grapes. In fact, the world's largest winery is in the San Joaquin Valley: the E. & J. Gallo Winery in Modesto. And with the cost of vineyard land in the north coast counties of Napa and Sonoma rising, many winery owners have shifted their sights here, replacing longtime pastureland with premium wine grapes.

Strawberry Shortcake with Cornmeal Biscuits

TOPPING

3 cups (12 oz/375 g) strawberries, hulled and sliced

4 tablespoons (2 oz/60 g) sugar, or to taste

fresh lemon juice to taste

1 cup (8 fl oz/250 ml) heavy (double) cream

¼ teaspoon vanilla extract (essence)

BISCUITS

1½ cups (7½ oz/235 g) unbleached all-purpose (plain) flour

½ cup (2½ oz/75 g) yellow cornmeal

1 tablespoon baking powder

1 tablespoon sugar

½ teaspoon salt

2 tablespoons chilled unsalted butter, cut into small pieces

about 1⅓ cups (11 fl oz/340 ml) heavy (double) cream

Berry growers love the gentle, ocean-moderated climate along California's midcoast near Watsonville, Monterey, and Santa Cruz. The beautiful strawberries grown here are shipped around the country.

1. Preheat the oven to 425°F (220°C). Line a heavy baking sheet with parchment (baking) paper.

2. To make the topping, in a large bowl, combine the strawberries and 3 tablespoons of the sugar, or more to taste. Let stand for 15 minutes, then half-crush the strawberries with a potato masher to release more juice. Add the lemon juice and set aside. In another bowl, whisk together the cream, the remaining 1 tablespoon sugar, and the vanilla until soft peaks form. Cover and refrigerate until needed.

3. To make the biscuits, in a bowl, stir together the flour, cornmeal, baking powder, sugar, and salt. Cut in the butter with a pastry blender or 2 knives until the mixture resembles coarse meal. Add the cream gradually, stirring with a fork until all the flour is moistened and the mixture begins to come together. Knead briefly by hand in the bowl until a soft, moist dough forms that you can remove in a single mass.

4. Turn out the dough onto a lightly floured work surface and knead gently 3 or 4 times to make a cohesive dough that you can roll into a shape. With a lightly floured rolling pin, pat or gently roll the dough into a rectangle about 5½ by 8 inches (14 by 20 cm) and about ¾ inch (2 cm) thick. Cut into 6 equal squares and transfer to a baking sheet.

5. Bake until well risen and lightly browned, about 22 minutes. Split the warm biscuits in half horizontally. Put each bottom, split side up, on an individual plate. Spoon the berries and berry juices over the bottoms, then top with a generous dollop of whipped cream. Cover with the top biscuit halves. Serve immediately.

SERVES 6

NUTRITIONAL ANALYSIS PER SERVING
Calories 587 (Kilojoules 2,465); Protein 7 g; Carbohydrates 55 g; Total Fat 39 g; Saturated Fat 24 g; Cholesterol 137 mg; Sodium 474 mg; Dietary Fiber 3 g

Glossary

Almonds
These nuts were brought to California in the mid–18th century by the Franciscans, who planted almond trees at the 21 missions they established from San Diego in the south to Sonoma in the north. The trees, however, did not thrive in the cool, moist coastal climate along the mission route, and it was not until the early 20th century that an almond-growing industry established itself in the Central Valley. More than 450,000 acres (182,200 ha) of almond orchards are now under cultivation, and California produces 100 percent of the nation's and more than 70 percent of the world's commercial crops of this mild, sweet-tasting, crunchy nut.

Anchovy Fillets
A tiny relative of the sardine that once thrived off California's coast, the anchovy is most often enjoyed in the form of salt-preserved, oil-packed fillets that lend briny flavor to everything from Caesar salads to pasta sauces to pizzas. Look for anchovy fillets in well-stocked food stores or Italian delicatessens.

Arugula
Prized for the refreshing nutty taste of its dark green, spear-shaped leaves, this traditional Italian salad green, also known as rocket, is produced by many small growers in California, who guarantee a steady supply to food stores and farmers' markets.

Asian Greens
One vivid sign of the continuing Asian influence on California kitchens is the widespread availability of Eastern produce, especially Asian greens. Among the most commonly found varieties are bok choy, pungent baby mustard greens, and tat-soi, a relative of cabbage, whose small, spoon-shaped dark green leaves with long, handlelike white ribs explain its occasional English name, spoon cabbage.

Capers
These small gray-green buds of a Mediterranean evergreen bush are commonly preserved in salt and sold packaged in either salt or vinegar for use as a zesty garnish for appetizers or salads or as a flavoring in sauces.

Cheeses, Imported
Besides the many locally produced artisan cheeses (page 32), a variety of imported cheeses plays an important role in the California kitchen. Some Italian examples used in this book are mascarpone, a thick, almost fluid, slightly soured cream cheese, most often used in desserts or to enrich sweet or savory sauces; and Parmesan, prized for its pale amber color, almost crystalline texture, and salty, nutty flavor, the result of careful aging for at least two years. This cow's milk cheese may be appreciated as a grating cheese or in small chunks or thin shavings as a complement to appetizers, salads, or fresh fruit. Those imported products labeled Parmigiano-Reggiano are considered the finest. Pecorino, a tangy Italian sheep's milk cheese, is best known in its aged grating form, of which the two most popular types are pecorino romano and pecorino sardo.

Chiles
Hot chiles, which entered California from Mexico with the Franciscan padres in the 18th century, were long associated with the cooking of the border states. In recent years, Southeast Asian cooks have added their own passion for chiles to the state's melting pot. Modern California cooks can make use of many different types of chile to enliven their cooking,

including the plump, small jalapeño, a very hot variety found in both its unripened dark green and, less commonly, its ripened red forms; the rich-tasting poblano, usually sold dried; and the small, slender, very hot green or red serrano, sold fresh, and used in many Asian- as well as Latino-inspired dishes.

Coconut Milk, Unsweetened

A growing interest in Southeast Asian cooking has made canned unsweetened coconut milk a key ingredient in the pantries of many California cooks. Like nonhomogenized cow's milk, coconut milk separates, forming a thick layer of cream on top. For this reason, canned coconut milk should be shaken before use. You can also spoon off the cream for using on its own in recipes calling for coconut cream, or discard and use the balance of the can for lower-fat versions of recipes calling for coconut milk.

Crème Fraîche

Literally "fresh cream," this typical French product, now widely available in California, is in fact a lightly soured cream used in both sweet and savory dishes. Crème fraîche may be stirred into sauces or other preparations as an enrichment and does not curdle like sour cream. At its simplest, a chilled dollop may be spooned atop fresh fruits such as berries.

Eggplant, Asian

Also variously known as the Japanese or Chinese eggplant (aubergine), this variety of the vegetable fruit is distinguished by its slender shape, measuring as long as eight inches (20 cm) and no more than about two inches (5 cm) in diameter. It is most often the familiar eggplant purple or lavender, although some rare varieties

Herbs

BASIL
In addition to common fresh sweet basil, a favorite year-round Mediterranean seasoning, look for the highly aromatic Asian or Thai basil, distinguished by dark green leaves on purple-tinged stems.

BAY LEAVES
Despite their availability, leaves of the California variety of the bay laurel tree are considered to have too pungent and assertive a flavor for cooking; imported bay leaves are preferred. Be sure to remove the dried leaves from dishes before serving.

CHIVES
Available throughout the year, these thin green shoots provide a mild onion flavor.

CILANTRO
Also known as Chinese parsley or fresh coriander, these bright green leaves of the coriander plant deliver a pungent—and pleasing—flavor.

DILL
This feathery, sweet herb is a natural partner to seafood, particularly the salmon that is so popular in California.

HERBES DE PROVENCE
This commercial herb blend typically includes rosemary, thyme, and savory, along with such other signature seasonings of Provence as oregano, basil, lavender, and fennel seed.

MINT
With its cool, fresh taste, mint—of which the most commonly sold culinary variety is spearmint—is used in a wide variety of both savory and sweet dishes from Europe, North Africa, India, and Southeast Asia.

OREGANO
This robust Mediterranean herb finds ample use in California, reflecting both Italian and Mexican influences on the state's cooking.

ROSEMARY
This highly aromatic Mediterranean herb may now be found growing wild in parts of the state. It complements grilled meats.

TARRAGON
With its delicate perfume reminiscent of anise, this classic French herb flatters eggs, seafood, green beans, asparagus, and poultry. It is frequently infused in vinegar for use in sauces or salad dressings.

may be found with green or ivory skins. Available year-round but at peak of season in spring and summer, Asian eggplants are appreciated for their lack of bitterness and big seeds sometimes found in their larger globe-shaped cousins. Stored in the vegetable bin of the refrigerator, the eggplant will remain in good condition for up to 1 week.

Fennel, Bulb

Resembling a squat, bulb-shaped head of celery, this Mediterranean vegetable, with its crisp texture and refreshing anise flavor, has found favor in California's sunny climate. Bulb fennel may be eaten raw, thinly sliced in salads or appetizers, and is also good sautéed, grilled, steamed, or braised as an accompaniment for seafood or chicken. The delicate, dark green fronds may be used as a seasoning in the same way as those of a related type of fennel grown specifically as an herb.

Fish Sauce

The most common savory kitchen seasoning in Southeast Asian kitchens, this thin, clear, brown liquid is made by fermenting a small, anchovylike fish. Several different nations have their own more-or-less interchangeable styles and names for fish sauce, including the *nam pla* of Thailand and the somewhat milder and more delicate-tasting *nuoc mam* of Vietnam.

Focaccia

Similar to a risen but untopped deep-dish pizza, this old-fashioned, Italian-style flat bread has become a popular item in California's boutique bakeries.

Lemongrass

A common seasoning in Southeast Asia now also grown in California and other parts of the United States, this stiff, reedlike grass has a sharp flavor reminiscent of citrus. Look for fresh lemongrass in ethnic and farmers' markets and well-stocked food stores. The best flavor comes from the heart of lemongrass, reached by peeling away the tough outer leaves down to the stalk's inner pale purple ring. Lemongrass is usually chopped or bruised to release its fragrant oils.

Mushrooms

Enterprising growers keep California cooks supplied with a wide selection of mushrooms, including many now-cultivated types that were once only available wild. In addition to white- or brown-skinned common cultivated mushrooms, popular varieties include creamy gray, fan-shaped

Oils

BASIL OIL

Olive oil in which fresh basil leaves have been infused to form a flavorful seasoning for salad dressings, marinades, or sauces.

OLIVE OIL

Hands down the most popular cooking oil today, olive oil is pressed from the fruit of the olive tree (page 43). Although regular, blended, and filtered olive oil is widely used for sautéing and other cooking purposes, extra-virgin olive oil, a rich, fruity oil made from the first pressing of the olives, extracted without use of heat or chemicals, is widely appreciated as the finest of all the olive oils.

PEANUT OIL

This oil is particularly prized by Chinese and other Asian cooks for the rich taste it imparts and because it may be heated to high frying temperatures without smoking.

SESAME OIL, ASIAN

Although natural-foods stores sell pale sesame oil pressed from untoasted seeds for general cooking purposes, Asian cooks most often employ a dark amber oil pressed from toasted sesame seeds, adding it as a rich seasoning to sauces, soups, and stir-fries. Good-quality brands are imported from China and Japan. Buy in small quantities and store in a cool, dark place, as the oil goes rancid quickly.

TRUFFLE OIL

Olive oil richly scented with shavings of French black or Italian white truffles may be used sparingly to add an earthy aroma to dressings and sauces.

WALNUT OIL

Look for oil pressed from lightly toasted walnuts, for use as a seasoning or in salad dressings. Buy in small quantities and store in a cool, dark place, as the oil goes rancid quickly.

oyster mushrooms, whose taste and texture are thought to evoke the shellfish from which they take their name; and large, flat-capped, circular portobello mushrooms, enjoyed for their robust, almost steaklike taste and texture. Noncultivated types include gold- or apricot-colored, trumpet-shaped chanterelles, with a subtle, slightly peppery flavor; and meaty morels, with their conical, dark brown, honeycombed caps.

Oranges

Although the size of California's orange industry ranks second to Florida's, California leads the citrus-producing states in fresh orange production. Southern California's navel orange is sweet, juicy, and virtually seedless. It takes its name from the distinctive navel-like indentation at its blossom end. California's second most grown orange is the Valencia, which, although it can be eaten out of hand, is primarily a fresh juice orange. Another variety of orange grown in Southern California is the blood orange, named for the light- to deep-red blush of its peel, flesh, and juice. Native to Sicily, the blood orange is prized not only for its startling color but also for its intense, sweet flavor.

Persimmon, Fuyu

Now grown in California and harvested in the autumn, this Asian persimmon variety looks like a pale tomato. Unlike the more common Hachiya persimmon, the Fuyu is at its best when eaten crisp, like an apple.

Rice, Arborio

With a rice industry that began only as recently as 1909 in Sacramento Valley paddies irrigated by mountain waters from the Sierra Nevada and Cascade ranges, California has developed extremely advanced methods for growing this essential grain. Today, the state produces more rice per acre than any other nation in the world. Some California-grown rice, notably that carrying the CalRose label, has medium-sized grains and ample surface starch comparable to the Italian Arborio variety, used to make the creamy risotto dishes so popular today.

Saffron Threads

These hand-picked and dried stigmas of a particular variety of crocus flower are one of the world's most precious spices, contributing bright golden color and highly aromatic bittersweet flavor to seafood, chicken, and rice dishes. Use only saffron threads, the whole dried stigmas, rather than powdered saffron, which dissipates in flavor more quickly and may be adulterated.

Soy Sauce

A flavorful, salty liquid fermented from soybeans and some form of grain, usually wheat, soy sauce is one of the most common seasonings in China and Japan. The popularity of the cooking of those nations has led to its widespread use and availability in California. Chinese cooks use two types of soy sauce: dark, which is aged longer and includes a touch of molasses, is usually added to more robust dishes such as these featuring red meat; while light soy is most commonly used in dipping sauces and soups and with seafood and vegetables. Japanese soy sauce contains a higher percentage of wheat and is actually closer in color and flavor to Chinese light soy sauce.

Tomatoes

After Florida, California is the second most prolific commercial grower of tomatoes in the United States, with approximately 40,000 acres (16,200 ha) under harvest from May through mid-November. While the state's large-scale farmers concentrate on a few familiar varieties, boutique growers and home gardeners are rediscovering the pleasures of so-called heirloom varieties, tomatoes long ago dropped from mass production because of picking and storage limitations but prized today for their unusual sizes and shapes, colors—some variegated, some not—and exceptional flavor.

Vinegar

With its booming wine industry, California also produces outstanding red and white wine vinegars. Look in well-stocked markets and specialty-foods shops for varietal vinegars, which will exhibit some of the same distinctive flavor characteristics as their namesake wines. Besides locally made wine vinegars, other vinegars favored by California cooks include sherry vinegar, which echoes the richness of the fortified wine, and balsamic vinegar, a specialty of the area around Modena, Italy. Based on condensed grape juice, aged and reduced for years in a succession of ever-smaller barrels made from different aromatic woods, balsamic vinegar develops a heady sweet-sour flavor and an almost syrupy consistency.

Walnuts

Close to 100 percent of the walnuts sold in the United States are grown in California, which also produces approximately two-thirds of the world's walnut supply. Although walnuts are an autumn harvest, they keep extremely well. In their shells, the nuts stay fresh for up to three months under cool, dry conditions. Once shelled, the nutmeats will keep in an airtight container for up to six months in the refrigerator or a year in the freezer.

Index

Acknowledgments

Leigh Beisch wishes to thank the Cowgirl Creamery, Point Reyes, CA; and Farella Vineyard, Napa, CA. She also wishes to thank The New Lab and Pro Camera, San Francisco, CA, and FUJI Film for their generous support of this project.

Weldon Owen wishes to thank the following people and associations for their generous assistance and support in producing this book: Desne Border, Ken DellaPenta, Dana Goldberg, Niki Krause, Andrea Lewis, Annette Sandoval, the California Avocado Commission, Heath Ceramics, Hill Nutrition Associates, and Naomi's.

Photo Credits

Weldon Owen wishes to thank the following photographers and organizations for permission to reproduce their copyrighted photographs:
(Clockwise from top left) Pages 14–15: Olaf Beckmann; Rachel Weill; Lisa Romerein; Miki Duisterhof; Laurie Smith; Richard Bowditch; Laurie Smith
Page 16: Lisa Romerein; Leigh Beisch; Lisa Romerein; Rachel Weill
Page 50: Laurie Smith; Eika Aoshima/Janet Botaish group; Laurie Smith; Richard Jung
Page 86: Lisa Romerein; D.C. Lowe/FPG International; Laurie Smith; Lisa Romerein; Rachel Weill
Page 120: Andy Freeberg; Rachel Weill; Rachel Weill; Laurie Smith; Andy Freeberg

Time-Life Books is a division of Time Life Inc.

Time-Life is a trademark of Time Warner Inc.,
  and affiliated companies.

TIME LIFE INC.

President and CEO: **Jim Nelson**

TIME-LIFE TRADE PUBLISHING

Vice President and Publisher: **Neil Levin**

Senior Director of Acquisitions
  and Editorial Resources: **Jennifer L. Pearce**

WILLIAMS-SONOMA

Founder and Vice-Chairman: **Chuck Williams**

Associate Book Buyer: **Cecilia Michaelis**

WELDON OWEN INC.

Chief Executive Officer: **John Owen**

President: **Terry Newell**

Chief Operating Officer: **Larry Partington**

Vice President International Sales: **Stuart Laurence**

Managing Editor: **Val Cipollone**

Copy Editor: **Sharon Silva**

Consulting Editor: **Norman Kolpas**

Design: **Jane Palecek**

Production Director: **Stephanie Sherman**

Production Editor: **Sarah Lemas**

Food Stylist: **George Dolese**

Prop Stylist: **Sara Slavin**

Studio Assistant: **Sheri Giblin**

Food Styling Assistant: **Leslie Busch**

Scenic Photo Research: **Caren Alpert**

The Williams-Sonoma New American Cooking Series
conceived and produced by Weldon Owen Inc.
814 Montgomery Street, San Francisco, CA 94133

In collaboration with Williams-Sonoma
3250 Van Ness Avenue, San Francisco, CA 94109

Separations by Bright Arts Graphics (S) Pte. Ltd.
Printed in Singapore by Tien Wah Press (Pte.) Ltd.

A WELDON OWEN PRODUCTION
Copyright © 2000 Weldon Owen Inc. and
  Williams-Sonoma Inc.
All rights reserved, including the right of
reproduction in whole or in part in any form.

Map copyright © Ann Field

First printed in 2000
10 9 8 7 6 5 4 3 2 1

Library of Congress
Cataloging-in-Publication Data

Fletcher, Janet Kessel.
California / general editor, Chuck Williams; recipes and
  text by Janet Fletcher; photography by Leigh Beisch.
    p. cm. — (Williams-Sonoma New American Cooking)
    ISBN 0-7370-2039-3
    1. Cookery, American--California style.   I. Williams,
Chuck. II. Title. III. Series.
TX715.2.C34 F59 2000
641.59794—dc21   99-43384
                    CIP

A NOTE ON NUTRITIONAL ANALYSIS
Each recipe is analyzed for significant nutrients per
serving. Not included in the analysis are ingredients
that are optional or added to taste, or are suggested
as an alternative or substitution either in the recipe
or in the recipe introduction. In recipes that yield
a range of servings, the analysis is for the middle
of that range.

A NOTE ON WEIGHTS AND MEASURES
All recipes include customary U.S. and metric
measurements. Metric conversions are based on
a standard developed for these books and have
been rounded off. Actual weights may vary.